DESIGN MATTERS //
# PORTFOLIOS 01
AN ESSENTIAL PRIMER FOR TODAY'S COMPETITIVE MARKET          MAURA KELLER

BEVERLY MASSACHUSETTS

ROCKPORT PUBLISHERS

First published in the United States of America by
Rockport Publishers, a member of
Quayside Publishing Group
100 Cummings Center
Suite 406-L
Beverly, Massachusetts 01915-6101
Telephone: (978) 282-9590
Fax: (978) 283-2742
www.rockpub.com

**Library of Congress Cataloging-in-Publication Data**
Keller, Maura.
  Design matters : portfolios 01 : an essential primer for today's competitive market / Maura Keller.
     p. cm.
  Includes index.
  ISBN-13: 978-1-59253-602-3
  ISBN-10: 1-59253-602-6
  1.  Art portfolios--Design. 2.  Graphic arts--Marketing. 3.  Design services--Marketing.  I. Title.
II. Title: Portfolios 01.
  NC1001.K45 2010
  741.6068'8--dc22

                                                                        2009040599
                                                                        CIP

ISBN-13: 978-1-59253-602-3
ISBN-10: 1-59253-602-6


10 9 8 7 6 5 4 3


Series Design: CAPSULE
Book Layout: Megan Jones Design


Printed in China

# Contents

# INTROD

# UCTION

"IT IS A LAW OF HUMAN NATURE THAT IN VICTORY EVEN THE COWARD MAY BOAST OF HIS PROWESS, WHILE DEFEAT INJURES THE REPUTATION EVEN OF THE BRAVE."
—GAIUS SALLUSTIUS CRISPUS

THE SHOEMAKER'S CHILDREN HAVE THE WORST SHOES IN TOWN. AN AGENCY'S CAPABILITIES BROCHURE IS IN DIRE NEED OF UPDATING. YOUR RECENT HOLIDAY MAILER ENDED UP WISHING EVERYONE A HAPPY FOURTH OF JULY. LET'S FACE IT: YOU NEVER GET A CHANCE TO WORK ON YOUR OWN PROMOTIONS. IT ISN'T A GOOD EXCUSE TO SAY YOU'VE BEEN TOO BUSY TO SELL YOURSELF, BECAUSE WHEN YOU FIND YOURSELF WITHOUT ENOUGH WORK, YOU'RE A DAY LATE AND A DOLLAR SHORT.

# The Art of Portfolio Design

Portfolios. They are the classic sticky wicket. If you do them right, you will thrive. If not, you can lose money and potential customers. And for many businesses, portfolios and self-promotions can cause the biggest headaches. The good news? Using the right mix of your own ingenuity while highlighting your creative prowess can expand your clientele and improve your bottom line.

So how do you stand out in a crowd? Perhaps you carry a polka-dot umbrella that screams "notice me." Or maybe you don a more subtle approach to self-promotion—flashy socks that are quietly hidden under standard-issue khakis.

Find your voice. Drop those meager attempts at getting noticed and start to toot your own horn. Really toot it. Of course, shouting, "I'm the greatest creative professional out there. Hire me!" may not get you very far, but if you learn the art of self-promotion and make it your own, the results may surprise you.

# Get Competitive

## DON'T JUST SURVIVE–THRIVE

Marketing, advertising, and promotions are vital components of most companies' business plans, and creative professionals are no exception. The right portfolio mix and the shape it takes can enhance your ability to make a name for yourself in the industry.

In today's competitive marketplace, designers must compete to survive. And yet some creatives believe that simply putting a few cardboard business cards in the hands of prospective clients is their best marketing tool. Others would like to utilize stronger, more impactful portfolios so that they can entice more clients to join them in conversation. As part of the marketing mix, portfolio development and promotions can make a critical contribution to a firm's ability to achieve its objectives.

The bottom line, frankly, is that self-promotion is necessary to survive. The most successful design firms and creative individuals find ways to market themselves in ways that are memorable and that resound with their audiences. In order to be competitive in the future, you should be doing the same.

The Creative Group, a firm that specializes in placing marketing, advertising, creative, and Web professionals on a project basis, polled 250 advertising and marketing executives about the importance of building a strong portfolio. They were asked, "Which of the following do you consider most important when hiring a creative associate?"

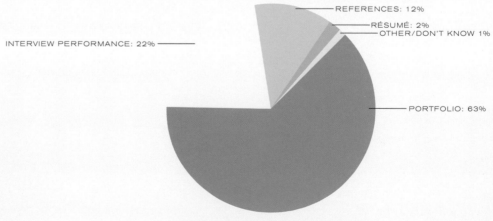

REFERENCES: 12%
RÉSUMÉ: 2%
OTHER/DON'T KNOW 1%
INTERVIEW PERFORMANCE: 22%
PORTFOLIO: 63%

SOURCE: *BOOK SMARTS* BY THE CREATIVE GROUP

THE O GROUP
259 W 30 STREET / NYC 10001
T/ 212.398.0100  F/ 212.398.9191
WWW.OGROUP.NET

259 W 30 STREET / NYC 10001

THE D GROUP

▲ *The main objective of The O Group's portfolio update was to appear sleek enough to appeal to their luxury-focused clients, while showing off a winning personality. The firm's portfolio is a permanent hardbound piece, supplemented by modular "mini portfolios" that can be printed on demand in their office and bound, DIY-style, with a sleek rubber band. Carefully considered simplicity was the guiding principle for the design—the restrained palette and sparse layouts afforded a lot of freedom to express themselves with creative typography and copywriting.*

THE O GROUP

# The Master of Your Domain
## THE IMPORTANCE OF GETTING FOUND

Experienced designers agree that besides being willing to take creative risks, successful creative professionals share a common trait: persistence. It's the name of the game for portfolio design. Persistence is what makes us try again and again in the face of rejection and setbacks.

Bottom line: The responsibility of self-promotion and getting your portfolio in the hands of the right people rests with you. If you can't pay your electric bill this month, guess whose fault it is? If your portfolio doesn't impress your prospective client, then you probably won't get their business.

The good news is that portfolio development is easier than it looks—and not always an expensive proposition. It can be a viable growth strategy—even a survival tactic for your business. Here's why:

**Portfolios get you noticed.** Portfolio development isn't just for the big guys, and it doesn't have to cost much. In fact, some of the most memorable portfolios are often the ones that exude a simplified approach to showcasing who you are and what you bring to the proverbial table.

**Portfolios add to your credibility.** Nothing says, "I have the experience to get the job done" better than an impressive portfolio. It shows work you've done for your clients and how you've impacted their businesses with design. Talking the talk can only get you so far. You need to let your prospects' fingers do the walking as they turn the pages of your brochure, or click on your PDF portfolio, which they received only moments earlier.

**Portfolios garner a level of respect.** Find a niche and start scratching. For one demographic, a funky leave-behind piece may be the best medium. For another, a memorable holiday mailer may do the trick. Be sure to do your homework and determine what your target audience will respond to. It could mean the difference between hitting the mark and missing the target.

**Portfolios build your confidence.** Creating portfolios that truly illustrate your creative genius can instill tremendous confidence to individuals or firms. Even in those moments when you are lacking the creative genius that you were sure you had, you can glance at your portfolio and say, "I did it once, I can do it again."

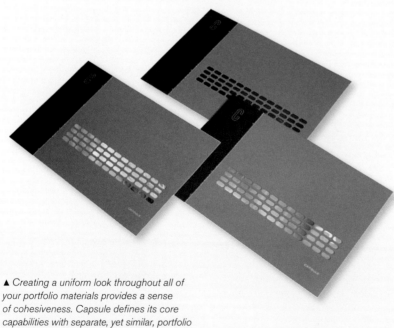

▲ Creating a uniform look throughout all of your portfolio materials provides a sense of cohesiveness. Capsule defines its core capabilities with separate, yet similar, portfolio components that appeal to clients interested in different facets of the firm's products and services.

CAPSULE

▲ Personalized promotions help define who you are in the minds of your clients. They can surprise, excite, and tell a story about your creative capabilities. From monogrammed cashmere scarves to handcrafted jewelry to personalized stationery, promotions are sacred gifts that clients look forward to receiving.

The Fusion Hill design team created both women's and men's stationery sets that included eight different notecard designs, gift enclosures, and a memo pad. Printed digitally on uncoated stock using Fusion Hill brand colors, each piece within the set was monogrammed with the client's first initial. Sets were then packaged and tied with a bow. One hundred personalized sets were created and hand delivered.

FUSION HILL

# The Essence of Portfolio Design

## Q&A WITH NEIL TORTORELLA

Neil Tortorella has more than thirty years of experience as an award-winning graphic designer, writer, and marketing consultant. He has operated his own design and marketing consulting practice, Tortorella Design, for more than twenty years.

**Q: WHAT IMPORTANCE DOES A PORTFOLIO PLAY IN THE BUSINESS OBJECTIVES OF BOTH INDEPENDENT DESIGNERS AND FIRMS OF ALL SIZES?**

A: Ideally, the portfolio should focus on work that the designer or firm is good at creating, enjoys creating, and is the type of work they want to do.

Talent is, or at least should be, a given. The truth be told, there are scores of very talented designers out there, but they should focus on their strengths in their self-promotions. For some, logos come easy, but designing a website is like pulling teeth. For another, brochures are a piece of cake, but designing a logo gives them an anxiety attack. It's important to play to one's strengths and do a bit of soul-searching to find out what one is really good at doing. We create our best work when our heart, soul, and mind are into it and enjoy working on it.

Talent, execution, and even enjoyment aren't quite enough if there isn't a market for it. It's important to research what clients are buying, what's profitable, and build on what you like to do, then find ways to tailor your portfolio to that market and its needs.

**Q: WHAT ARE THE CORE ELEMENTS THAT YOU FEEL ALL PORTFOLIOS SHOULD INCLUDE?**

A: A portfolio should be more than a simple collection of designs. It should tell a story. A well-thought-out book should flow with a logical beginning, middle, and end. And like all good stories, the beginning should grab attention; the middle fills in the details and builds to the climax.

A portfolio should start with a great, memorable piece and end with one. Selecting them can be tough. Some things to keep in mind are:

- Is it flawlessly executed and produced?

- Are the message and design clear and captivating?

- Did it fulfill the goals of the project?

- Does it reflect the type of work you want?

- Does it reflect your personal style?

Whether you mount your work or slide it into acetate sleeves, ensure that everything is clean, square, and without bent corners. The substrate should be neutral and take a backseat to the work. I've seen too many books with mattes and mounting methods that outshined the designer's work.

Make sure the case is clean and doesn't look like it was made in 1942, unless it's supposed to look like it's from 1942. The case is the first thing a prospect sees, and it sets the stage for the presentation.

Find a way to make your portfolio stand out. This is especially important for drop-off versions. That might mean a custom case or a clever, yet functional, way to mount the pieces. If it's mounted, be sure all work is mounted on a standardized board such as 16 × 20 inches (41 × 51 cm) or 20 × 24 inches (51 × 61 cm). Different-size boards are distracting and awkward.

**Q: WHAT ROLE DO SELF-PROMOTION ITEMS PLAY IN THE DESIGN INDUSTRY TODAY?**

A: Self-promotion is extremely important for all designers—those seeking employment at a firm or agency and those drumming up work as a freelancer or business owner. A savvy, smart promotional plan and strategy can separate the "haves" from the "have-nots."

There are a lot of very talented designers out there, so employers and clients have a lot of choices. It's the ones who are remembered that usually get the jobs. A less-talented creative with more visibility can outshine a more talented designer with less visibility.

The designer's promotional toolbox should contain a variety of elements beyond the portfolio. These can include mailers such as postcards and brochures, stationery, websites, blogs, newsletters, press releases, networking, speaking engagements, and writing articles. The trick is finding the ones that work well for you and that you can manage over the long haul. Marketing is about consistency over time. One-shot deals don't often make a career.

**Q: HOW OFTEN SHOULD DESIGNERS PROMOTE THEMSELVES IN A COMPREHENSIVE MANNER?**

A: Designers should do some form of marketing, at the very least, weekly. That can take the form of emailing a useful link or two to some prospects and clients, posting to their blog, attending a networking event, or writing a press release.

Mailings should be monthly to quarterly. Longer than every three months or so and your name will fade, and you'll find yourself starting over or at least playing catch-up. Conversely, mailing too often, aside from getting expensive, can be construed as desperate and annoying. Prospects can become numb to your mailings pretty quickly.

Postcards are often an inexpensive way to keep in touch and show off some new work. But it's easy to get lost in the postcard shuffle. I get a lot of them from photographers and illustrators that, at best, get a brief glance on the way to the garbage can. If you choose to do a postcard campaign, give it some quality thought. It needs to stand out from the crowd and immediately grab a prospect's attention. The same holds true of email promos and enewsletters.

◄ *Clean Design's brochure serves as a stand-alone self-promotion piece as well as an introduction to Clean Design's new branding. It was created to support the firm's belief in the effectiveness of design and their position as a strategic firm with extensive branding capabilities. The leave-behind includes an overview of their design philosophy and their structure and process, as well as a sample portfolio.*

CLEAN DESIGN

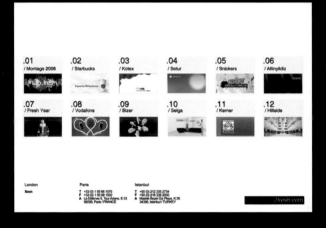

It's also important to test the waters. Creatives can get too close to their work, and emotions can get involved. Run your promotional items by some trusted colleagues and, even better, some clients. Get as much feedback as you can before you spend a lot of money on something that might be off target.

**Q: DURING YOUR CAREER HAVE YOU SEEN ANY PORTFOLIOS OR SELF-PROMOTION ITEMS THAT HAVE TRULY WOWED YOU OR THE AUDIENCE AT LARGE?**

A: I've been in the business for over thirty years. I've seen several great portfolios and, unfortunately, a lot of mediocre and even lousy ones.

One designer, in particular, stands out. His work was utterly brilliant. The presentation was flawless. It was a 20 × 24-inch hard case with the work mounted on black foam core board. He had cut triangles out of each board to make it easy to pick each piece up. The cutouts also lent a sense of interest and geometry to his portfolio. The point is that I remember him and his portfolio, and that meeting was over twelve years ago.

**Q: HOW CAN TODAY'S IN-NOVATIVE MARKETING TOOLS, SUCH AS BLOGS, PAY OFF FOR CREATIVE INDIVIDUALS OR FIRMS WHO ARE LOOKING TO "GET THEIR NAME OUT THERE"?**

A: I do a lot of marketing consulting for creatives. My blog is naturally about marketing and self-promotion for that target audience. Marketing seemed like a logical fit. When I started my blog, I didn't really know what blogging was all about. Truth be told, I started it because a client wanted me to design one for them. I figured I'd better learn quickly. Within three months of starting up, my site traffic tripled.

▲ *Since websites are updated often and advertising works disappear quickly in the digital world, 2Fresh shows video presentations of their projects. These annual Showreel DVDs provide quick snippets of each project completed by the firm within a designated year.*

*2FRESH*

**Q: WHAT ARE SOME KEY MISTAKES YOU'VE SEEN DESIGNERS AND/OR FIRMS MAKE WHEN IT COMES TO PORTFOLIOS AND SELF-PROMOTION?**

**A:** All too often, portfolios and self-promotions tend to be self-serving instead of serving the audience. Designers can easily gravitate toward viewing their work and promotional endeavors from their point of view rather than what's important to the prospect.

Another problem area is showing too much. It's better to present a handful of great pieces than loads of mediocre ones.

Also, I believe it's important for designers to show their thinking skills, such as showing thumbnails, roughs, and comps along with the finished material. Again, it's that storytelling bit. "Here was the client's problem. This was my thinking process, and this is the final solution."

Research is yet one more important thing. It's a huge help to learn all you can about a target industry—this will set you apart from your competition. More than likely, you'll find common problems and challenges that can be addressed in various promotional items. With research comes marketing ammunition. It enables a designer to speak with authority in their marketing communications, but also address points that are truly important to the audience.

When you do these things, it's much easier to be in control of a portfolio review and have something more useful to say than, "I thought this was a kick-butt font, and I really like PMS 200." Although an art director might agree, they're more interested in what the results were and how you got there.

◄▼ *This presentation of selected case studies is housed in a compact workbook. The layout of the media is based on 804 Graphic Design's own corporate design and is found throughout the firm's other communication materials.*

804 GRAPHIC DESIGN

# PLANNI

# NG

"THE CULT OF INDIVIDUALITY AND PERSONALITY, WHICH PROMOTES PAINTERS AND POETS ONLY TO PROMOTE ITSELF, IS REALLY A BUSINESS. THE GREATER THE "GENIUS" OF THE PERSONAGE, THE GREATER THE PROFIT."

—GEORGE GROSZ

WANT TO ILLUSTRATE THAT YOUR CREATIVE TENDENCIES ARE FAR-REACHING AND ENCOMPASS A MYRIAD OF DESIGN RATIONALES? PROVE IT. ARE YOUR LOGO DESIGNS DEFINED BY UNIQUE TYPOGRAPHY AND COLOR CHOICE? SHOW IT. CREATE PROMOTIONAL ITEMS THAT ARE JUST THAT, PROMOTIONAL. SHOW YOUR TRUE COLORS. BRAG. FLAUNT YOUR STUFF LIKE A BIG, BLOOMING PEACOCK.

# The Big Picture

We've all seen them: portfolios and self-promotions that seem to have a life of their own. Teeming with well-designed, innovative graphics, these portfolios are not the cookie-cutter renditions of yesteryear. Rather, they are streamlined masterpieces that stand out in the minds of a targeted audience.

Remember when you were a kid and your mother used to say, "If you can't say anything nice, don't say anything at all"? These days, many people espouse an updated version of that philosophy: "If you can't build a portfolio right, don't build it at all." Portfolios are core marketing tools, and the statement they make by their appearance and functionality is critical to the business they represent.

Planning your portfolio, namely what form it will take, the contents within, and to whom it will be distributed, is the first step in portfolio development. This stage of the process will allow you to step back and see the big picture in terms of how you want your portfolio to impact you and your company. Do you want your portfolio to be a permanent symbol of who you are and what your company does, or do you want it to be customizable to each recipient? Should your portfolio content include visual as well as verbal components, such as case studies, that will clearly define your creative vision? Or perhaps the visual components of your portfolio should simple speak for themselves. As with all things design, take your time to get it right and remember the adage, "Planning makes perfect."

# Sleek and Chic

## A LITTLE BLING GOES A LONG WAY

▼► *Choosing a sleek portfolio with simple, well-defined imagery and minimal copy draws the viewer in. A silver cover with coordinating bright orange vellum inserts is a defining characteristic that is carried throughout b-on creative's engaging portfolio.*

B-ON CREATIVE (SOUTH KOREA)

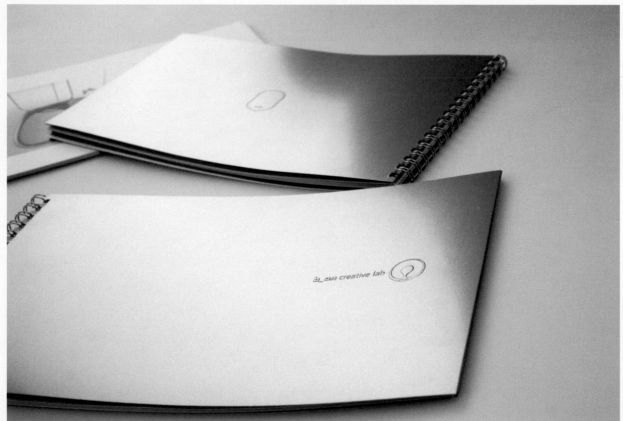

# Taking the Bull by the Horns

MAKING YOUR PORTFOLIO WORK FOR YOU

In the past, designers and creative firms commonly approached marketing and self-promotion in an uncoordinated fashion, with portfolio development relegated to the lowly status of being addressed only after the garbage was taken out—if then.

While creatives play a huge role in the global economy, these individuals and firms find themselves reinventing their marketing techniques to compete in a saturated market.

So how do the best creative firms create portfolios and self-promotion campaigns that make targeted clients comfortable enough to loosen their purse strings? Portfolio design and self-promotion can be a relatively simple matter: Take examples of your existing product or service and let a particular group know you're there to serve it—albeit in a fun and unique way.

Conversations with experts produced a list of old-standby practices that, with a couple of unique twists, make for a lucrative portfolio campaign. Among those practices are evaluating how your portfolio fits in the market and crafting an appropriate message ensuring that you leave a lasting impression.

In fact, one of the most difficult problems facing many businesses is establishing a promotional strategy that is profitable, logical, and competitive.

Determine your marketing objectives, which will result in different promotional strategies. For example, your promotional objective might be one (or all) of the following:

- Increase sales

- Increase your customer base

- Maximize long-term profits

- Stay competitive

- Establish a stronger market position

You need to understand your competition by keeping abreast of what the guys down the street are doing in terms of portfolios and self-promotions. Find out what is working for them and what is not. Then create your own strategy.

But remember: Simply deploying a series of promotions or designing a stand-alone portfolio isn't enough. Although strategic use of promotions has proven to be a good system for some designers, it is important that it is not the quick fix. Instead, it should be a coordinated effort between your marketing and sales functions.

◄▲ *The portfolio of Lockstoff Design is cleverly bound together with a single metal rivet, which makes it attractive and functional. When fanned open, recipients can see a snapshot of several projects the firm has worked on. The opposite side of each fan leaf offers detailed information about the project on the front. The single fan leaves are interchangeable, offering a flexible way to update the portfolio when necessary.*
LOCKSTOFF DESIGN

# EIGHT TACTICS FOR PORTFOLIO DESIGN

··· **A PICTURE IS WORTH A THOUSAND WORDS.** Include more visuals and less verbiage on your promotions. The visuals should tell the story.

··· **MAKE IT MEMORABLE.** "A memorable portfolio is the key to a successful designer. A good designer must know his audience, and one step further, must know the target market," says Marshall Haber, president of Marshall Haber Creative Group. "We get dozens of portfolios every week from designers looking for work. The ones that stand out demonstrate quality and cohesiveness. The last thing I want is a designer that is all over the place. If showing quality means showing less, I'm fine with that.

"I look for design that communicates and motivates rather than just design for design's sake. Bells and whistles in design are great, even necessary, but they need to enhance a project, not overtake it. Our business essentially services clients in sales, so the reality is that our work has to inspire action. I never forget that my job is to communicate a message for our clients clearly and effectively. When I see a portfolio that demonstrates that understanding, it stands out as a winner."

··· **TIMING IS EVERYTHING.** Timing a promotional campaign is an art. Marketing is 99 percent good timing. Synchronize your portfolio design to back up a direct-mail or email campaign. Promotions that appear out of nowhere, with nothing else to support them, usually do not generate the desired results.

"Digital technology makes customization easier. It also means that work can be sent across the globe in seconds," Haber says. "I've hired a freelancer within minutes of getting a portfolio via email. If you got the goods, you'll make an easy sell."

··· **IT'S A BALANCING ACT.** Whatever the method, a good promotional strategy is determining frequency, reach, and timing. The decisions you make about these three factors will determine how your portfolio campaign is weighed.

"The main purpose of creating a portfolio is to show the quality of your work. Exquisite work is a designer's best asset," Haber says. "An equally important part of any new business presentation is providing a prospective client with case studies and sales figures of previous jobs. That's what helps to land the account. Portfolios aren't just important to a designer or a design firm, they're essential. If you want to claim your territory as a great designer and distinguish yourself in one of the most competitive creative industries out there, take your PDF and stick it in the ground."

··· **A COMPLEX FORMULA.** One thing we know from tapping the heads of consumers of creative services is that portfolios and self-promotions alone are rarely the primary motivator in selecting a creative professional. That's true whether you're in a high-, medium-, or low-price niche, a large firm or a one-person shop. The selection process is part of a complex formula rooted in how customers know and understand your experience, your credentials, and the products and services you offer—both in terms of quality and confidence.

"Portfolios that speak to the target are very powerful," Haber says. "Digital technologies make it easier to customize a presentation or portfolio for each target. That's not a unique trend so much as it is a smart trend, and technology has made customizing easier. Something that doesn't work is complexity. I've seen portfolios and presentations that seem to go everywhere. The key word in good design is focus. A designer must also have a sharp business sense and a planned strategy."

··· **MARKETPLACE KNOW-HOW.** Your promotional strategy should be continually evolving. Strive to take the continuing pulse of your marketplace, creating your own

scenario of how your portfolio can capture the attention of your audience, and revising your promotional strategy accordingly to help maximize your profits.

"Technology has dramatically transformed the nature of portfolio presentations. Today, portfolios are either sent as PDFs or as website links," Haber says. "Virtual portfolios allow the client to interact with the work, and more importantly, with the designer. Obviously, this shift demands a different and wider skill set. Classic black cases and spiral flipbooks are not totally obsolete, as I'll often present a new client with a hard copy of the portfolio at our initial meeting as a tangible reference of our scope and capabilities. It is therefore critical for a good designer to have both digital and print skills."

··· **DEMOGRAPHICS, HERE WE COME.** Getting to know the demographics of your potential customer base, including their purchasing power, can greatly enhance how well your portfolio is received.

··· **PARTNERS IN PROGRESS.** Tap into your existing client base—many of whom may be more valuable than you realize. The beautiful thing about having an accurate database of existing and former clients is that these people know other people. And assuming you offered a gratifying client experience, there is no reason that your old clients wouldn't refer your offering to potential new clients—especially upon seeing an updated portfolio.

# Defined Design

▼▶ *Carefully selected images and a clear vision that walks viewers through each page is at the heart of this portfolio book. "The book is intended to work as a personal portfolio for potential clients," says Nikolaus Schmidt. "The overall intention is to show clients the diverse production techniques that can be achieved." Featuring commercial as well as personal projects, the images shown on the French-folded pages are clearly defined with clean visuals. The blue inserts feature a thicker stock with the key facts of each project including client name, date, and kind of work.*

NIKOLAUS SCHMIDT GRAPHIC DESIGN

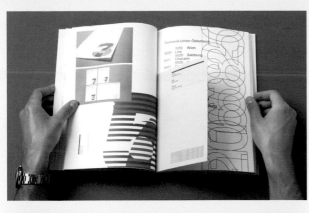

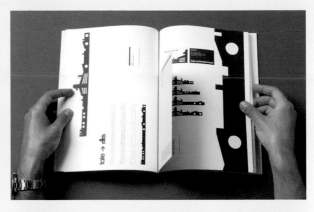

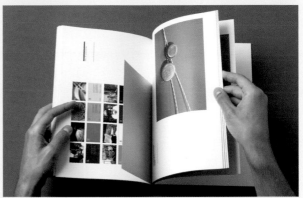

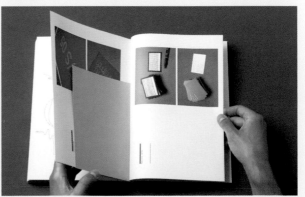

# The Medium Is the Message

## NO ONE SAID YOU HAVE TO FOLLOW ONE PATH ON THE ROAD TO SUCCESS

Good portfolio design is a critical element in attracting potential prospects. Your content is your greatest lure—no tricks or gimmicks, just the goods. You've got a story to tell, so tell it. But *how* you tell it is as important as *what* you tell. Marshall McLuhan has long been known as the man behind the message—the coined phrase, "the medium is the message." In his book *Understanding Media*, McLuhan asserts that "the form of a medium embeds itself in the message, creating a symbiotic relationship by which the medium influences how the message is perceived."

If you determine that the best medium for your portfolio is a whiz-bang CD filled with interactive elements, perfect. Or perhaps a traditional printed portfolio that showcases your firm's work is more suited to your designated audience.

Better yet, maybe simple, straightforward e-blasts will get your message across. The medium that you choose to display your work needs to reflect who you are as a creative professional. In declaring "the medium is the message," McLuhan goes one step further to propose that the media itself, not the content it carries, should receive the most attention. However, in the creative world of design, the content of your portfolio is a vital component of showcasing who you are and what you do. The medium should grab their attention and usher them inside—eager to find out more.

The medium in which your portfolio or self-promotion piece is housed can be the most memorable component. Whimsical, fun, knock-your-socks-off-creative—that's what will get you noticed.

► *These portfolio cards were designed like mini case studies, showcasing various facets of Brand Engine's most notable work. Each card gives a glimpse into the stages of brand development, the breadth of the projects, the assorted applications of the brands, as well as some contextual placements. The goal was to create a system that would be convenient to customize and print in-house and easily mailed or carried for quick hand-offs at meetings. The result? A color packet of cards strategically designed to create a memorable impression of what Brand Engine is all about.*

BRAND ENGINE

At Brand Engine, we specialize in designing successful, sustainable consumer brands through strategic rigor and insightful creative expression.

It's what we do best.

# Finding the Right Mix

## PERFECT INGREDIENTS, PERFECT PORTFOLIO

Remember back to the good old days of kindergarten when you couldn't wait to grab the attention of your fellow comrades with the beloved show-and-tell? At the ripe old age of five, you knew that it is far more powerful to "show and tell" than to just "tell."

The same holds true for portfolios and self-promotion.

Indeed, a lot of designers may say, "I tried it and it didn't work." And to that, the little person in your head should respond, "You tried it and it didn't work as well as you wanted *that* time." Who's to say a similar self-promotion piece won't woo a potential prospect the next time around? You just need to make sure there's going to be a "next time."

"Never underestimate the obvious," says Andrea Cutler, professor of design at Parsons School of Design and owner of Andrea Cutler Design. "Your portfolio, along with a well-designed and organized résumé, and good cover letter are *you*. They're the first impression. And a great business card for networking is critical. If you are a designer, especially a freelancer, then that single item alone speaks volumes about your capability. I never go anywhere without my cards. I also have a mini business-card-size 'port-a-folio' on a key chain, that I make on a need-be basis to give people. They are an effective marketing tool for me."

andrea
cutler
design

calif.949.679.2895   nyc.212.316.0788   cell.917.287.1686
andrea@andreacutler.com

◄► *A key chain–size mini portfolio offers a great leave-behind piece for potential clients to take with them and share with others.*
ANDREA CUTLER DESIGN

With well-designed portfolios, you feed the passion. You create aficionados. The way you do that is to get them in the proverbial "door" with other aficionados—your "followers"— the ones who keep coming back for more.

Create your own fan club. Educate them about who you are and what you can do. You want to fuel the passion, fuel the flame. And portfolios and self-promotions are absolutely the most cost-effective way to do it.

Of course, zeroing in on the potential audience most likely to respond to your portfolio is essential. This is achieved through choice of media, position, or placement, along with the messages your self-promotion delivers. The more you are "front and center," the more they will remember you and your capabilities.

# Ideas at Work

## DON'T FORGET TO LEAVE THE LIGHT ON

So what are some portfolio techniques that really work? Some people say tangible portfolios (versus the virtual ones) and self-promotions are a waste of money—it's word of mouth that sells *you*. Others feel that it is the total communications mix—and the appeal of your creative know-how—that really sells. One thing is for sure: By putting your portfolios in front of your target audience, across a variety of communication channels, the message begins to strike home.

A good portfolio strategy also is a balancing act between targeting frequency, reach, and timing. The decisions you make about these three factors will determine how your promotional campaign is weighed. But the form your portfolio design takes is also paramount. Whether you choose to create traditional portfolios housed in the standard sleek black case or nontraditional portfolios, such as magazines or PDFs, you need to make sure form and function meet.

▶ *Based in Bologna, Italy, LLDesign creates their self-promotional portfolio by including selected works from the last four years. Measuring 17 × 24 cm (6.7 × 9.4 inches), this portfolio is digitally printed on different kinds of paper and hand bound. It's a great example of how the form the portfolio takes complements the function of the design elements within.*

LLDESIGN

# OUT OF THE MOUTHS OF THOSE ON THE FRONT LINES OF DESIGN

For many creative professionals, how you format your portfolio is dependent on how long you've been in the creative business and what you see as the best way to showcase who you are and what you do. Andrea Cutler, professor of design at Parsons School of Design, asked a variety of colleagues and students, some of whom have been in the design industry for decades and others who are "wet behind the ears," how they format their portfolios. Here's what they had to say:

"I am just taking my first baby steps in graphic design, and since I already want to apply for different jobs, I decided to use a blog temporarily to show my humble portfolio pieces."

"As with any portfolio, if you're going to show your work, your blog needs to look first class. Just like a website, don't present it until the medium itself is a portfolio piece."

"I have an online portfolio. If requested, I send a PDF, which I also have on my website. I have a book that I show when I get invited for an interview so that I am able to speak about my body of work in person."

"I've been a designer for five years, and I still have an 11 × 17-inch [28 × 43 cm] book, but I also have my website, and other online profiles that allow for a portfolio gallery."

"My initial contact is always my website. Sometimes it's email, sometimes phone, and sometimes a self-promo, but always the website."

"I am still using the same formula I have used since I graduated from art school ten years ago: a traditional book on the smallish side [11 × 17 inches; 28 × 43 cm] and a PDF for emailing and online samples. I send the PDF most often. I have never been asked for a leave-behind book nor have I mailed one to a client, agency, or studio. I have gotten most jobs networking."

"I have been in business for twelve years now (in-house and freelance), and the way I refer to my work is via PDF, on my website, and with a custom book. When I first started out, I had the standard black leather book with samples attached."

"I have been a graphic designer for over twenty-three years. I originally used a traditional book with vinyl pages, but now use a hard case with individual boards and mounted images and a few hard copies of brochures, etc."

"I've been practicing for over twenty-eight years. I used to drop off a physical portfolio. Now I use only my website with downloads and direct mail support."

▲◄ *"As a graphic designer whose expertise is in print, it is important for me that my portfolio reflects my abilities in this discipline. Therefore, I chose to display my design pieces in a book. I selected the most outstanding case studies that I had created in the past few years. The layout is simple, clean, yet keeps the viewer engaged, as there's still a lot of movement inside the spreads. The focus is always on the images, whereas the text is used as a complementary—and balancing—element."* Carmit Haller

CARMIT DESIGN (BELMONT, CALIFORNIA)

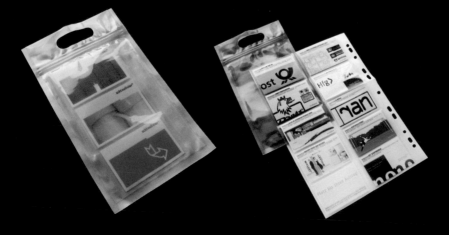

◄ This self-promotional package of business cards uses the small dimension to showcase an intriguing miniature portfolio on the back of each card. The extraordinarily colorful packaging in the form of a little bag provides the bling-bling needed to grab the viewer's attention.

804 GRAPHIC DESIGN

# Portfolios and Brand

## A SYMBIOTIC RELATIONSHIP

Many a provider of goods and services would like to do for their business what Starbucks has done for the coffee shop—get the consumer or client to spend about three times what they used to spend. It is not that their coffee is so superior, although it is very good. Rather, it's their innovative marketing. Starbucks has transformed the ordinary task of getting something to drink into a delightful experience. And it resonates throughout their brand.

Experts define brand as every prospect or customer interaction with your company that creates an impression. But a corporate or product brand is clearly more than just a logo or an advertisement—it's the personality and soul of a company. When it comes to branding your portfolio, there are some common mistakes to avoid:

- **Inconsistent messages.** A good self-promotional campaign is dependent upon consistency to build trust and strength in a message. For example, let's say your portfolio features an award-winning website followed by an outdated logo design for a company that's no longer in business. Having such inconsistent design elements featured in your portfolio can send a wrong message about who you are and where you're taking your company.

- **Failure to differentiate.** Creativity is the key to differentiation. And creating a unique position for yourself and your company provides a solid foundation for your brand.

"Your brand is defined by other people's perceptions," says Karl Speak, president of Brand Toolbox, an organization that helps companies and individuals define their brand. Speak is also the former chair of the board of directors of the Design Management Institute, a nonprofit, global organization dedicated to demonstrating the strategic role of design in business and to improving the management and utilization of design. "Strong brands are perceived to be distinctive, relevant, and consistent. The most distinctive brands are perceived to make the biggest difference."

For example, if you fail to distinguish yourself at a trade show, by offering a standard candy-dish-topped booth display, you fail to give potential customers a reason to select you rather than the gal next door. Simply put—make every meeting and event memorable in the minds of your audience. Have creative stand-alone portfolio items that you can hand out at a moment's notice. Create surprise and delight at every turn. That's what differentiation is all about.

- **Inconsistent, ineffective identity.** A brand is everything from how your phone is answered to the quality of your customer service to the content of your blog, not to mention your company logo, office interior, and marketing materials—it's critical that each of these elements appropriately represent your company's identity. If one or more of these elements is inconsistent with the total message, you are confusing your audience. Make sure your identity is consistent. A strong brand is the result of good experiences, consistent messages, and positive, reinforcing images. "The process of building a strong brand is to define your brand platform and deliver on your brand promise," Speak says.

▲► A strong level of brand consistency is evident throughout Gerard Design's portfolio and self-promotional pieces. The "You'll See" piece was developed to support the agency's rebranding. Treating itself as a client, Gerard Design took a research-based approach that ultimately highlighted the need for sweeping changes to the core facets of its brand, including repositioning itself as a strategic branding firm (not just design), refining its messaging to clearly communicate the agency's capabilities, and creating a visual identity that consistently supports Gerard Design's image and culture.

The "You'll See" piece is a mini portfolio targeted toward new and potential clients to demonstrate the company's branding abilities. Using a coated paper highlights the photography and images, which together emphasize the company's high-end work. In other words, the firm lets the images do most of the talking.

GERARD DESIGN

warm
holiday
wishes

chilly

gerard design

# CREATI

# NG

"SUCCESS CAN MAKE YOU GO ONE OF TWO WAYS. IT CAN MAKE YOU A PRIMA DONNA, OR IT CAN SMOOTH THE EDGES, TAKE AWAY THE INSECURITIES, LET THE NICE THINGS COME OUT."

—BARBARA WALTERS

BE A BIG FISH IN A LITTLE POND. BE A LITTLE FISH IN A BIG POND. IN AN AGE WHERE "ANYTHING GOES," IT TAKES A LOT OF COMMITMENT TO DEFINE YOURSELF. LET YOUR LIGHT SHINE THROUGH. LET YOUR EXPERIENCE AND EXCITEMENT ABOUT YOUR WORK SHOW. BEHOLD YOUR COMPETENCY AND MAKE SURE YOUR PORTFOLIO IS ALL DRESSED UP WITH SOMEPLACE TO GO.

TAKE A GOOD LOOK AROUND.
WHAT DO YOU SEE?

# Lather, Rinse, Repeat

To find work, you must look for it actively. This means promoting yourself. "I'm not a salesperson," you might insist. But the truth is, to grow your business, you're forced to wear a sales hat. You need to talk about your company and what you do. You have to be the walking, talking billboard of your company, with your portfolio in hand.

Experts agree that you need to structure your portfolio's content so that it is the most meaningful to those whom you have identified as your key audience. Strive for brevity, while also telling a story. For viewers who want more details, provide expansive case studies of your work.

# Streamlined for Success

## KISS—KEEP IT SIMPLE, STUPID

When evaluating your vision for your portfolio, ask yourself:

When your audience looks at your portfolio or self-promotion piece, do they quickly find what they are looking for? Are they engaged with what they see? In general, most don't, and they back out faster than they would when they leave a bad movie.

Here's where the tough part comes in. Engage with your audience and determine what is working and what is not. What information should you have in your portfolio and what can be omitted? Let's face it: every person is different and their response to your portfolio or self-promotion may be different from the next guy's. But if there is a consistent thread of discontent with your portfolio—such as not enough visuals or your copy does not meld with the visual creativity you espouse—pay attention. If you are repeatedly asked for clarifying information after a recipient has viewed your portfolio, take note and make the appropriate changes that will garner the response you are looking for.

Most expert advice on portfolio design can be summed up in a single word—simplicity. This may sound almost trite, but simplicity is key when it comes to developing a consistent, memorable portfolio or self-promotion.

In addition to simplicity, a well-thought-out portfolio strategy will go a long way. As in the early world of computing, it was often said that a computer is only as good as the programmer—"garbage in, garbage out"; the same can be said of portfolio design.

The bottom line? A focused, powerful portfolio will set you apart from the competition, break through the clutter, accelerate relationship-building, and dramatically improve your probability of success.

◄▲► *1977 Design created their portfolio showcasing nine case studies that demonstrate the skill sets of the studio. Instigating dialogue and engaging with the recipient was the drive behind the portfolio design, as they looked to use this as an opportunity to express the studio's personality and ethos. "An approachable tone of voice was created that used the logo as the lead-in for all headlines of the brochure," says Richard Stevens, designer at 1977 Design. The company name was given a variety of suffixes to create the headlines. "Client testimonials were featured next to each project, breaking down the barriers that design fluff sometimes creates," Stevens says. "This allowed us to communicate our design approach in a manner that wasn't arrogant or mundane, focusing on engaging the recipient. The '1977 Designed this' line is now used as a crediting logo for any work coming out of the studio."*

1977 DESIGN

# Portfolio Must-Haves

## KNOWING WHEN TO STOP AND WHEN TO GO

Jeff Fisher, founder of LogoMotives and author of *The Savvy Designer's Guide to Success: Ideas and Tactics for a Killer Career*, provides insights for creating that perfect portfolio.

### Be creative! That's now your job.
Don't simply present potential employers with a standard student portfolio. When portfolios from local schools are reviewed, many contain the same class projects and begin to look exactly the same. Incorporate some individual projects—perhaps some real-world work for a nonprofit organization in which you have a strong personal belief.

### Keep actual book size manageable.
A large and unwieldy portfolio case is going to make for an awkward and less-than-favorable first impression with an interviewer. Keep it small, concise, and manageable so as to not knock items off the desk of a portfolio reviewer.

### Be concise.
Maintain a limited number of pieces in your book and make sure the work is your BEST. Include unique pieces that showcase your talents and skills. Most creative directors and art directors will not have much time to review a large amount of your work. Showcase your very best work first, keep the number of included projects small, and make the most of the time you are given for the presentation.

### Have a fine-tuned spiel.
Saying "and then I designed this, and then I designed this…" as you turn the pages of your book will not make a great impression. Clearly explain the brief, your process, and any defined results for each project included. Having a process or sketchbook available for review is a great idea. Practice your presentation with friends, family, or student peers before a presentation for a comfortable and polished presentation.

### Be honest about your work.
Be up front about your participation in any collaborative project effort rather than claiming full credit for the job. Show only your own work in your book. You will be caught if attempting to misrepresent yourself. The design community makes up a very small world.

### Make use of online portfolios.
The Internet provides incredible—and often free—resources for showcasing your work and creating easily accessible websites.

### Social networking is your self-promotion/marketing friend.
Many of the current Internet social networking/media sites provide great opportunities to network with potential employers and showcase your work in a gallery.

# Portfolio Expectations

## TEST YOUR KNOWLEDGE

The Creative Group surveyed 250 advertising and marketing executives about what they expect in a portfolio. See if you know the answers.

① What is the percentage of executives polled who value overall creativity most when evaluating a portfolio?

Answer: ................

② What is the average number of items executives recommend should be included in a portfolio?

Answer: ................

③ What is the number of samples typically viewed before determining whether someone is qualified for the job?

Answer: ................

④ What is the number of people within a firm who typically evaluates a candidate's portfolio before a job offer is extended?

Answer: ................

⑤ What is the number of work samples that executives expect to see in an online portfolio?

Answer: ................

⑥ What is the percentage of executives who, on average, spent five minutes or less reviewing online work?

Answer: ................

ANSWER KEY: ① 69 ② 11 ③ 9 ④ 3 or more ⑤ 9 ⑥ 33

# Content Is King

## LONG LIVE THE MOTTO: GARBAGE IN, GARBAGE OUT

When creating your portfolio, you need to find your niche and highlight the design components that fit your business and your experience. You know your product and you also hopefully know the people who need your product or service.

Do you embark on a treasure hunt of sorts, rummaging through every creative element you have ever developed? Certainly not. Determining the content of your portfolio should require deliberation and a fair amount of strategic thinking.

The first step in portfolio development is deciding which pieces warrant inclusion. Select items that are clearly representative of your skill base and

expertise. Keep in mind that some clients require permission to promote work that you've completed for them, so get written approval prior to creating your portfolio or self-promotion items in which their work will appear.

Depending on your level of expertise; be sure to include enough elements within your portfolio that capture the breadth of your creative genius.

◀▲ *A fourteen-page concertina showcases the company's portfolio. The concertina is divided into two sections, "Work" and "Play." The Work section features corporate projects, while the Play section features personal projects and work for clients who specialize in fun products and services.*

CREATIVE SPARK

## THE DO'S OF PORTFOLIO CREATION

⋯ Make it relevant. Your portfolio needs to be relevant to the audience. Include only those portfolio-worthy elements that really shine. Your portfolio should be streamlined, incorporating only the most pertinent examples of your work.

⋯ Make it timely. Ever walk into a doctor's office only to find an array of year-old magazines awaiting your perusal? No one wants to read old news. The same can be said for old portfolio content.

⋯ Make it understandable. There is no one standard way to organize a portfolio, but to be effective, it needs to be understandable and meaningful to your audience. Choose elements that provide a complete picture of your professional skills and abilities.

⋯ Remember that the documents in a portfolio are not meant to tell the whole story. Rather, the elements featured are intended to pique the viewers' interest and invite them to ask more questions.

# Design Parameters
## SHOWCASING YOUR CREATIVE CAPITAL

Artists, advertising creatives, designers, architects, photographers, fashion designers, and writers have been using portfolios as their primary promotional vehicle for centuries. Perhaps even Leonardo da Vinci had a portfolio of sorts when he was commissioned to paint the Sistine Chapel. A well-thought-out portfolio can be a very effective marketing tool—one that is imperative when landing that ideal job or next client.

According to Jeff Johnson, founder of Spunk Design Machine, today's high-end portfolios are efficient and very affordable to produce. That's because the advent of high-end, reliable, digital book printing and binding has really democratized the quality leave-behind portfolio options. "Companies like Bookmobile, Blurb, and others now provide excellent hard-bound, low-quantity, and low-cost book manu-facturing," Johnson says. This trend is also sometimes aptly called "vanity books," as they allow an independent designer or design student the option of designing and publishing a great hard-bound portfolio that can double as a leave-behind.

"That's on the good side of the fence," Johnson says. "On the bad side is the sole reliance on online portfolios to represent one's work. I regret this trend. A big part of the job of any good designer is lending distinction to the work at hand. The options for creating a lively, honest, and distinc-tive portfolio are endless. A website, however grand, is still just a website. I really cherish the care for the artifact. We live, and choose options, in a real 3-D world."

"On the sunny side, the Internet has really done a lot for democratizing ac-cess for designers. Internet access to design media has allowed our Spunk Design Machine to compete and succeed on a global scale," he adds.

"For a small boutique like ours, having a diverse client base is a must. Our online portfolio allows our work to travel where we can't, or won't. We have clients in Mexico, Switzerland, Ireland, Japan, etc. The smaller, cre-atively focused studios have a distinct advantage, as the barriers for delivery of quality of work have been radically eliminated in less than a decade. It's been a real game changer. Last year, we opened our first branch office in New York City. I had experienced a really difficult, and ultimately unsuc-cessful, design office expansion from Minneapolis to New York City with another great design company in the mid-'90s. The technical ease of our current studio expansion is due, in no small part, to the maturity of remote digital media access. Our clients can see our work in any number of cities and decide if our work is a potential fit. The remote studio option is just one more decision maker for the potential client," Johnson notes.

# THE DON'TS OF PORTFOLIO CREATION, BY JEFF JOHNSON

When I got into the design world after graduating in 1992, it was common to see some pretty mondo-crazy portfolio creations—mine being probably one of the worst and largest. The portfolio I brought to MTV, Push Pin Group, CSA, David Lance Goines, Duffy, etc., weighed in at 70 pounds—I'm not kidding. It even included a full 20 × 30-inch [51 × 76 cm] zinc plate,

and I manufactured my own carrying harness. I just had to have that hand-etched zinc plate, don'tcha know.

My second portfolio that I took to New Zealand in 1998 was only slightly less stupid. This one was made as a metaphoric handshake. The portfolio was an old powder-coated electrical switch box with a ceramic hand bolted

to the box. The hand was an old rubber glove mold I found at a surplus store. One could flip open the switch box and review the work. It mostly looked like a Trent Reznor nightmare. Today's portfolio model is an easy leave-behind piece that holds a DVD of more expanded work.

▲ ► *Two of the portfolios that Jeff Johnson utilized during the early years of his career— albeit memorable, they simply didn't offer the streamlined approach of today's portfolios.*

SPUNK DESIGN MACHINE

# It's a Digital World

## LET YOUR FINGERS DO THE WALKING

Websites say a lot about a company, so their appearance and functionality is critical to the business they represent. We all know that Web use has grown at a phenomenal rate and projections are higher yet. Even your plumber has his own website. You see the trend and know where you need to be. But how do you use the Web as a portfolio tool?

According to Neil Tortorella, marketing consultant and founder of Tortorella Design, technology and, in particular, the Internet, has had a tremendous impact on portfolios.

"It's a 24/7/365 world now," Tortorella says. "Art directors, employers, and clients can view online books at their leisure, search for exactly what they need (medium, style, specialization, etc.), and create their short list faster than ever."

The Web has also significantly increased the competition. There are numerous portfolio sites with scores and scores of portfolios. It's tough to stand out. Competition is no longer local, regional, or even national. It's international. Designers now compete, daily, with others across the globe who can often work for a lot less, while still producing good design.

According to Laura Hamlyn, creative director at Clean Design, online portfolios are simply expected these days. Even PDF versions of designer portfolios feel a little "analog."

"Earlier on, online portfolios were purely for convenience's sake—to ensure your work is easy to access," Hamlyn says. "Today, online portfolios serve as a way to showcase Web design capabilities. Clean Design uses our online portfolio as a way to showcase fresh work. It does not cost a thing to post new work online as often as we can."

Tortorella agrees: "On the upside, technology has made it possible to have your portfolio available online all day, every day." Digital media enables designers to easily distribute samples of their work. Plus, enewsletters, blogs, the myriad of social networking sites, along with sites like Flickr and Google's Picasa, have given designers a host of mediums to display their work to a larger audience. These outlets can, in turn, point to a designer's website, where visitors can see additional work or larger versions, read case studies, and learn more about the designer or firm.

Marketing and promotion via the Internet is easier and much more cost-effective than in the past. Sites such as Jigsaw.com and Spoke.com make finding targeted prospects a snap. Online press-release distribution services get a designer's news out to a broader audience, often for free. Business networking sites, such as LinkedIn.com and Biznik.com, keep people connected and offer them a vehicle to obtain introductions to prospects and promote themselves through their profiles, articles, answers to member questions, and such. Social networking, when used correctly, can also be a promotional tool. There's more to Twitter and Facebook than telling the world you're having a bad hair day.

"Add blogging into the mix and there's more opportunity," Tortella says. Blog topics can be case studies, how-tos, tips about working with a designer, or other design- and marketing-related content that would be helpful to both clients and prospects.

Beyond this, website and enewsletter traffic statistics help designers determine what content is important to prospects. This enables them to place promotional messages within a page's content or sidebar or help to drive traffic to other pages, as needed.

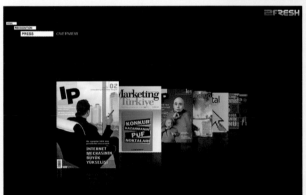

◀▲ *The website is one of the most essential tools of 2Fresh's self-promotion—especially while expanding to a new market like London. It provides a better format to express themselves and give in-depth information while maintaining the user's interest.*

2FRESH

# Showcase Showdown

## MAKE YOUR PORTFOLIO REALLY SHINE

Creative professionals have one thing in common—they strive to capture the attention of their potential audience through powerful visual messages. They want to make an impact on a viewer, to entice them to buy their product, attend their theatrical production, or simply marvel at the architectural prowess of a building. And for many, using digital elements can inform, delight, and inspire their audience like never before.

With each new day, technology brings exciting opportunities for growth and success. As businesses grow, designers encounter tough decisions regarding how to best use the technology available for portfolio development and self-promotion.

*◄▲ Housed in a beautifully etched metallic case, this promotional portfolio is where technology and traditional portfolio strategies meet. The metallic case contains a personalized metallic covered notebook, promotional CD, and a Velcro-enhanced folder, which includes a series of portfolio postcards.*

FACTOR TRES COMUNICACION

*► When sending email introductions, Monderer Design attaches a twelve-page promotional PDF. The PDF presents a mini portfolio of print, branding, and interactive design work.*

MONDERER DESIGN

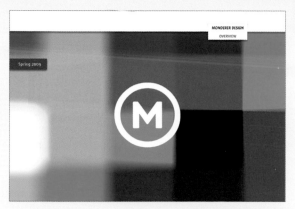

MONDERER DESIGN
OVERVIEW

Spring 2009

WORK
PRINT

> SolidWorks  Conference Branding

> Thermo Fisher Scientific  Advertisements

MONDERER DESIGN
OUR STORY

Monderer Design offers proven expertise in branding, identity, print, web and interactive communications for our clients. We specialize in defining and reshaping brands for today's changing marketplace.

Discover how our ⓜ-POWER™ methodology can help you transform your communications and transcend the competition.

WORK
BRANDING

belmont media center

> Belmont Media Center  Corporate Identity

> Ember Corporation  Literature System/Branding

> Informio  Literature System/Branding

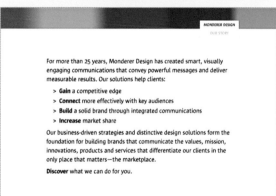

MONDERER DESIGN
OUR STORY

For more than 25 years, Monderer Design has created smart, visually engaging communications that convey powerful messages and deliver measurable results. Our solutions help clients:

> **Gain** a competitive edge
> **Connect** more effectively with key audiences
> **Build** a solid brand through integrated communications
> **Increase** market share

Our business-driven strategies and distinctive design solutions form the foundation for building brands that communicate the values, mission, innovations, products and services that differentiate our clients in the only place that matters—the marketplace.

**Discover** what we can do for you.

WORK
INTERACTIVE

> skoto  Web Site          > A.D. Makepeace  Web Site

> Stanley Rowin Photography  Web Site     > Language Weaver  Web Site

WORK
PRINT

> Fluent  Services Handbook

> Northeastern University  MBA Viewbook

MONDERER DESIGN
CONNECT

Thanks for your time.

For new business, general inquiries or the weather/traffic report from Porter Square, please contact us at:

Monderer Design
2067 Massachusetts Avenue
Cambridge, MA 02140-1337

tel  617 661 6125
fax 661 6126
stewart@monderer.com
www.monderer.com

# Interactivity at Its Best

## TOSS A WIDE NET TO CAPTURE YOUR AUDIENCE

Creative individuals and firms are quickly seeing the Internet as an essential tool for handling the "meat and potatoes" of day-to-day operations—including generating new customers; communicating with vendors and suppliers; improving visibility among prospective clients; and following industry trends online.

A professional website helps potential clients develop confidence and trust in a business. Websites provide a platform to spotlight your creativity at its best, as well as testimonials, case studies, and press coverage. A Web-based portfolio can give a potential client the confidence to pick up the phone and call, or it can send her clicking away. An effective online marketing strategy can expose a business to the world and reach new customers that might otherwise not even know it exists.

"It is important to design your portfolio with some context," says Laura Hamlyn at Clean Design. "Nothing is more frustrating than work that is too small to read or understand, cropped in a confusing way, or delivered without context. It is helpful to let people know how you were challenged or what types of obstacles your work was forced to overcome. I also like to see work 'in the wild.' Show your work in the context of where it is used, when applicable. That applies to packaging, environmental design, etc. Even if you are not an expert photographer, you can link to the more casual or personal photos of your work on Flickr."

Obviously, there is no face-to-face connection online. You cannot establish that personal chemistry that is essential to winning new business, so make sure your personality comes through in the style and writing on the site. Browsers should get a sense

▲ Simple, yet clearly defined imagery and straightforward project descriptions make TFI Envision's website one that is teeming with cohesive design and functionality.

TFI ENVISION

of who you are or the environment in which your firm operates. People with compatible personalities tend to work better together.

Keep file sizes small or use pre-loaders to ensure that your load times are quick and people can focus more on the work and less on how hard it is to look at it. Average wait times are just a few seconds, and then viewers grow impatient and move on.

A website must not only look attractive and function well, it must be easy to find. The best website in the world that nobody can find is like a magic trick in the dark. That's where all of the latest online marketing techniques such as search engine optimization, email marketing, RSS feeds, blogs, and podcasts come into play.

And like paper-based portfolios, Web-based portfolios contain all the elements that show the world who you are as a firm or individual. But remember, electronic portfolios are not for everyone. Be prepared to supplement your electronic version with a handheld paper version.

While some creative professionals rely solely on their website to showcase their portfolio, others try to engage their audience with PDFs and other interactive delivery methods.

▲ *This interactive PDF is an electronic exposé showcasing recent Spark Studio projects and success stories. The streamlined navigation system allows viewers to explore the interactive presentation via their own computer.*
SPARK STUDIO

▲ *From packaging to brand identity to environmental graphics, this interactive PDF document highlights Spark Studio's most recent work.*

SPARK STUDIO

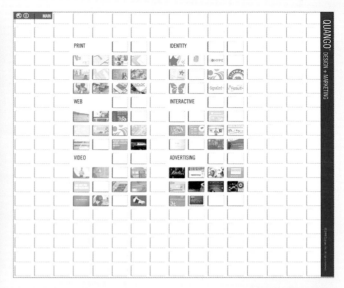

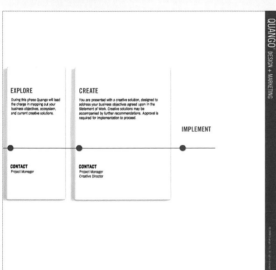

▲ *Walk into the Portland-based Quango office, and you'll see them on the walls—a diverse photo collage on 6 × 4-inch (15 × 10 cm) wooden blocks arranged in a matrix. For Quango, these grids foster inspiration. In their interactive portfolio, they encourage a similar experience for prospective clients. Built on an XML database, Quango's portfolios are highly customizable—allowing images and messages to be tailored to specific viewer interests. Dynamically pulling database content greatly simplifies updates while helping to ensure a relevant presentation of recent work.*

QUANGO

If updating your website or creating high-end interactive PDF portfolio presentations seems too daunting, why not try your hand at enewsletters—simple email blasts that are reminiscent of a press release, yet have the visuals and design elements to capture your audience's attention.

▲ *Using an ongoing series of e-news updates, Subplot Design celebrates recent projects and news with clients and prospects.*

SUBPLOT DESIGN

▲ *MMR Studio prides itself on ebrochures, both for their own marketing purposes and their clients'. To help support the firm's rebranding initiatives, MMR created collateral material including a CD presenter, business cards, and business card–size "flip folio."*

MMR STUDIO

# Nontraditional Portfolios

GIVE THEM SOMETHING TO LOOK AT *AND* HOLD

Are you the type of person who likes to go with the flow, or do you prefer to chart your own course in life—going against the current of all things mainstream? Perhaps you were the kid who ate peanut butter and banana sandwiches out of your dad's old lunchbox rather than consuming cafeteria cuisine on plastic trays. Being nontraditional certainly has its advantages. And in the creative world, nontraditional portfolios and self-promotions not only get you noticed, but they add to the overall memorability of your creative genius in the minds of your audience.

## SHOW YOUR TRUE COLORS

When you hand someone your capabilities brochure or latest self-promotion, do they say "cool" or just nod their head? You can easily measure your success with your portfolio by evaluating the response of your audience. Do they quickly flip the pages of your portfolio with thoughtless glances, or do they react with a "wow," or "that's impressive—tell me more." Be decidedly different.

That's exactly the mentality that Lawrence Everard, founder of Little Yellow Duck, espouses in his firm's portfolio strategies.

"There are a lot of tedious things in life, but top of the list has to be the traditional agency portfolio brochure," Everard says. "You know the sort of thing; '…a team of committed and experienced professionals… dedicated to the highest standards of creativity…results-focused and cost-effective…' and so it drones on, one earnest and completely redundant platitude after another."

Using humor and wit to create stories about yourself and your firm, along with a clever design, will draw potential clients in while demonstrating your creative abilities.

► "Little Yellow Duck and the Big Idea *was our attempt to show that charm, assurance, and a little wit would stand out from the crush of pompous agency philosophies that live out their short arc of life from drawing board to landfill via the client's wastepaper basket," founder Lawrence Everard says. "It was also a lot of fun to create, and that's important to us. Best of all, if you're the kind of client who likes the brochure, you'll like working with us, and if you don't, you won't. So it's not just a 'what kind of outfit are we?' brochure, but a 'what kind of client are you?' filter, too."*

Little Yellow Duck
and the
Big idea

A story for children and bright marketing folk.

## LITTLE YELLOW DUCK

"Once upon a time, a young art director was waiting at a photographic studio for some products to arrive for a shoot," Lawrence Everard says. "The products were late; the camera and the lighting were set up, and while they were waiting impatiently, the art director and photographer were casting around for a stand-in object to check the light levels. Eventually, the photographer's assistant found a little yellow plastic duck in the ladies' room, which proved to be the perfect subject for the test shot. That young art director always remembered how the little yellow duck had helped him out on that stressful afternoon, and years later decided it would make the perfect name for his own agency. And that's a true story… good night."

To be cost-effective *Little Yellow Duck*'s initial (and only) print run of the book was 1,000 copies. The attention and recall the book generates has been outstanding—many of the firm's contacts report that they receive new business promotions every day, but *Little Yellow Duck*'s is the one that really stands out.

delivery, then we know we will enjoy working with them. And we have been proved right. Making follow-up phone calls to check that the book has arrived is a joy. People remember it (and our name). The books have usually been passed around, and if we can get the receptionist on our side our job is almost done."

Albeit childlike, the illustrations complement the single message within *Little Yellow Duck and the Big Idea*. With a little help from your friends, your business is sure to succeed.

"The book makes it very easy to engage in conversation with prospects and for them to think creatively about solutions to their own communications," Everard says. "As a result, we attract clients who are willing to be brave with their own activity. The bonus is that if they are the type of client who enjoys this method of

Some have been sent to existing clients to pass around to friends and colleagues, while others have been used for prospecting. And, as Everard explains, the book has more than paid for itself in terms of business generated, from both new clients and new projects from existing clients.

One day, the little yellow duck had a visitor.

"Sorry I'm late" said the businesswoman. "I was trying to get Japan on my Blackberry."

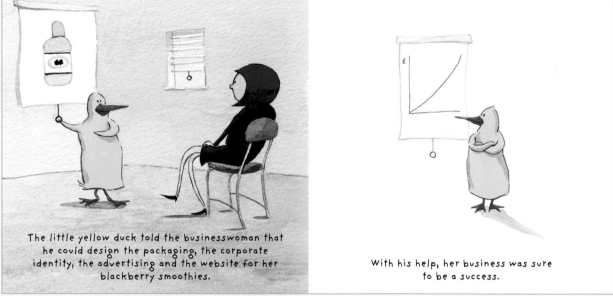

The little yellow duck told the businesswoman that he could design the packaging, the corporate identity, the advertising and the website for her blackberry smoothies.

With his help, her business was sure to be a success.

▲ This promotion was themed on Big Al's Farm Fresh Design—comparing the design industry to the chicken farming industry. The promotion included a screen-printed place mat; a wire spiral egg cup; a laser-engraved wooden egg, with teaspoon; plus a full-cover, French-folded booklet portfolio with a two-color plus white foil cover. All items were placed on a bed of wood wool (coarse, long wood shavings) inside a cardboard carton and finished with a custom-printed wrap.

LLOYDS GRAPHIC DESIGN (NEW ZEALAND)

▲ *Design Revolution in a can—themed around the Russian Revolution, with visual cues from that period of history, but some contemporary license in the design and typography—was an end-of-the-year promotion to thank clients. The tin included a candle, custom-wrapped chocolate cigar, and an A2 poster featuring various identities created by Lloyds Graphic Design during the previous year on one side and a call for designers everywhere to join the design revolution on the other. A printed tea towel features a tag that reads, "Unfurl this one-of-a-kind, custom-designed banner and show your true revolutionary colors to the world. Hold it high, walk tall and dare to resist the design despots who commit their crimes against our visual senses with impunity. Failing that, you can always dry the dishes with it."*

LLOYDS GRAPHIC DESIGN (NEW ZEALAND)

# Magazine-style Promotions Educate and Inform

Worrell Design recently created *New: For Lateral Thinkers* to tell stories of design and innovation from around the world. "Our vision is to raise awareness of global concerns that affect the design of business and the new roles of designers," says Kai Worrell. "We want to be recognized as a thought leader. We want people to be able to gain from the valuable insights we have uncovered as a company over the past three decades."

With eye-catching, colorful graphics and rich, meaningful collages of images pertaining to the articles, Worrell Design wants readers to be able to flip through the magazine and get a quick sense of the depth of the material, while creating a cohesive visual impact.

Every issue begins with a Founder's Note from Robert Worrell, followed by up to three interviews. The first issue included James McGregor, author; Joe Ranieri, chief executive officer of Crocs China; and Yu Shen, secretary-general of Shanghai Design Center. Each issue also includes case studies and articles written by Worrell Design research specialists.

Approximately 1,500 magazines were printed for the first issue. "We mailed and labeled the magazines in custom envelopes designed exclusively for that particular issue," Kai Worrell says.

And the response?

"People were incredibly impressed by the relevant, third-party content and overall quality," Worrell says. "They expressed appreciation for the knowledge we not only gathered and shared from third-party experts but from the direct information compounded from Worrell Design researchers and designers."

> Somebody growing up 5 years apart from somebody else is growing up in a different China because **THE PACE OF CHANGE IS SO FAST.**

◄▲ Worrell Design created a magazine to send to clients, featuring interviews and design case studies.

WORRELL DESIGN

# Self-Promotions

## IN THE DRIVER'S SEAT

No one can afford to send out multiple portfolio pieces throughout the year. Nor do you want to. Rather, consider accenting your portfolio with over-the-top creative self-promotions that really grab the recipients' attention.

By coordinating a "wow" moment with each self-promotion piece you create, you can dramatically enhance your portfolio strategy.

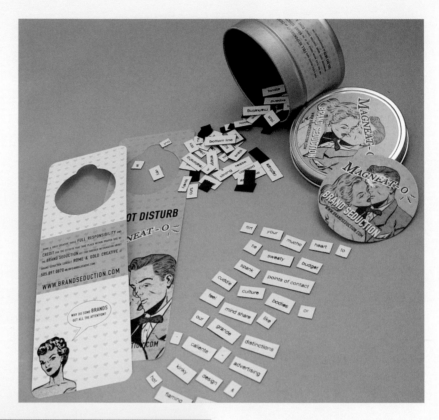

▲ Based on the attraction and seduction of good branding, Rome & Gold creative developed a refrigerator magnet kit that served as a novelty gift for the recipients. The magnets had branding and seductive words such as flaming, kinky, sweaty, and cuddle on them.
ROME & GOLD CREATIVE

◄ This self-promotion was wrapped around America's favorite pastime—baseball and hot dogs. The gift included an invitation, along with a nicely designed package of ketchup, mustard, and relish. Rome & Gold Creative also rented a suite at the local A farm team stadium and invited everyone out for a fun, casual evening of baseball, allowing them to strengthen their current relationships and to develop new ones.
ROME & GOLD CREATIVE

# HOLIDAY MAILERS

An excuse to do anything impressive— simply put, that's the reason holiday mailers are such a worthwhile effort. "Any significant holiday, and even the insignificant ones, offer an opportunity to show your passion, creativity, and thinking," says Aaron Keller, managing partner at Capsule. "Holidays also represent times of the year when mail has a better chance of being opened, considered, and perhaps even saved." But don't go down the holiday mailer chimney unless you have the talent to get your piece noticed and opened; you might find yourself stuck with a big bill and not much recognition to show for it.

▼ *"Some assembly required" is annoying on Christmas morning, but a welcome distraction in your office mailbox. This promotional mailer packed a promise to amuse, entertain, and for some, challenge.* CAPSULE

▲ Seasonality can be a great technique when it comes to self-promotions. These seasonal coasters were designed and printed via letterpress as self-promotional materials. They were sent out to clients on a quarterly basis. They also serve as leave-behinds after each portfolio presentation.

2 HATS DESIGN

▲ This small cardboard box was sent by freelance designer Steven Swingler to a variety of design agencies in East Sussex, United Kingdom. "Christmas Wishes from Steven Swingler" is stamped on the lid, and inside are polystyrene balls used for packing. When all the balls are removed, the recipient is rewarded with the message "Snowed under?"

STEVEN SWINGLER

◄ This box of real fortune cookies contained fortunes only Capsule could predict. Telling fortunes like "You're going to get up in the morning and go to work" and "You may find yourself inside an office building soon" was a humorous way to reach out to their client base.

CAPSULE

# face plot*

**Every year we give**
countless presentations, putting our
ideas and designs out there like
a lovingly-chosen holiday gift

And so
we've gotten pretty used to speculating on our
success by the audience reaction

**It's in the small details**
those that may otherwise go unnoticed
**that you find the truth**

You really need to scrutinize to get accurate results

Otherwise, you're just guessing,
aren't you?

With this easy-to-use pocket-sized set of flash
cards, you too can hone your expertise and
judge your own holiday gift-giving success rate.
Consider it your own little rosetta stone.

**Go on, try your luck.**
And see if you have the reaction-reading
abilities of a seasoned design team.

## euphoria*

\* Pure, unadulterated joy.

The contented smile, the slight wrinkles at
the eyes that convey genuine happiness
at receiving the perfect gift. It's what we all
aim for. We see this a lot, but if you need
help discerning this one, look in the mirror
as you're holding this card.

\* Subplot's self-administered test
**for gauging gift reactions**
this Christmas season

---

## feined gratitude*

\* Don't be fooled by the smile
and seemingly genuine twinkle
in her eye.

She's too grateful. No one is that grateful.
You know she just doesn't want to hurt your
feelings. But that gift will never be used.
Ever. This is often followed up by an overly
polite email explaining why a custom die, foil-
stamped, engraved, embossed and laminated
origami business card isn't within the budget.
Or in your case, asking for the gift receipt.

## wtf*
(what's the face?)

\* Look at those glazed-over eyes,
the blank stare, the slightly
drooping mouth.

Can you see it right? She is a virtual sphinx.
However, drawing upon our extensive
experience, we can tell you confidently that
this is the expression of elation. Or wrath.
It could be disappointment. There's a fair
chance that it's ennui. But more likely
exasperation. He's likely thinking "mmmm...
donuts." Or perhaps "is that guy's accent
real?" It's misery. Or potentially demoralization.
Irritation. Maybe heartbreak. Possibly revelation.
Or agony. Dashed hopes. Or repulsa.
Pure wretchedness?

---

▲► *Subplot strives to design a holiday card
that's not only a festive greeting but also a
useful guide to help navigate life. One year,
it was* The Truth Behind Design Jargon:
An Illustrated Manual; *another year, it was*
Trash to Treasure: Learn to Turn Spam into
Treasured Gifts.

*It's in the same spirit that Face Plot was
created. Subplot drew on their many years of
experience in deciphering the cryptic and often
unintelligible reactions of clients and suppliers.
Armed with this indispensable, handy set of
cards, you will never be in doubt as to what
they're thinking again, whether it's in a design
presentation or on Christmas morning.*

SUBPLOT

▼► *Each year Real Art Design Group creates a unique gift during the holiday season, and the 2008 gift took personalization to a whole new level. A set of cards showcasing the puppet version of the Real Art employees invited clients, friends, and family members to log on to A New Year, A New You and create a puppet version of themselves. The Real Art team then crafted the puppets and shipped them to their new homes neatly* packaged with instructions for completing the "new you" transformation. Keeping New Year's resolutions is never easy, but with the New You puppets, Real Art gave people the opportunity to accomplish their goals—even if it was through a puppet version of themselves. At the same time, Real Art was able to promote both their print and multimedia capabilities in a unique and fun fashion.*

REAL ART DESIGN GROUP

# Portfolio Components

## HOW YOU SHOW IT

"Curb appeal" isn't just for houses anymore. How you put your portfolio together—namely the materials used to house your portfolio—is often as important as what goes inside. Historically speaking, portfolios have traditionally come in two formats: books or binders. You know the ones—sleek black cases tucked under the arms or in the tight grip of creatives of all shapes and sizes.

Sometimes referred to as "show portfolios," these sophisticated renditions have garnered work for individuals and agencies alike. Remember, potential clients and employers get an immediate impression of you at first glance, so your portfolio format—both the exterior and interior—needs to be an extension of you or the company you represent.

Utilize a case that exudes professionalism and offers some distinction while reflecting the contents within. A custom case, albeit expensive, can be a perfect option. Local art supply stores also offer a wealth of innovative portfolio cases, binders, and boxes that may perfectly meet your specific portfolio needs.

Whether you mount your work or slide it into acetate sleeves, ensure that everything is clean, square, and without bent corners. "The substrate should be neutral and take a backseat to the work," says Neil Tortorella, marketing consultant and founder of Tortorella Design. "I've seen too many books with mattes and mounting methods that outshined the designer's work."

Make sure the case is clean and doesn't look like it was made in 1942, unless it's supposed to look like it's from 1942. The case is the first thing a prospect sees, and it sets the stage for the presentation.

Tortorella suggests you find a way to make your portfolio stand out. This is especially important for drop-off versions. That might mean a custom case or a clever, yet functional, way to mount the pieces. If it's mounted, be sure all work is mounted on a standardized board such as 16 × 20 inches (41 × 51 cm) or 20 × 24 inches (51 × 61 cm). Different-size boards are distracting and awkward.

# DIMENSIONAL KITS

The physical act of opening a box has symbolic relevance to the start of any new partnership. The act of giving a box or kit to a prospective client reveals what you are as a firm or individual—giving a brief glimpse into how you do what you do.

Creating a box is a personal effort, and it really shouldn't be mass-produced. When a box is delivered, it should feel like it was created for that individual within that company. If it feels like a template and that you just dropped off three others around town, the resulting effect on the participant will be lessened. This requires a production and assembly method that balances personalization with efficiency.

Finding a stock box and making it your own is a place to start—or make your own. Whatever is designed, it should offer the chance to be consistently produced with the optimal efficiency in production and personalization. Not all boxes stay inside the box.

Capsule has created many forms of the box or kit idea in their experimentations to find the match for their brand. From a small metal box lined with green fur to a handmade wooden box with pencil holes, Capsule has found that these kinds of promotions make a lasting impression.

▲ The wooden box was created for a multibillion-dollar toy manufacturer. Only two of these boxes were created, and they were hand-delivered to summarize a large presentation. The result was a significant amount of work from this toy manufacturer and a lasting relationship.

*The green fur box was created using leftover materials from two clients: The fur came from a client that produced stuffed animals, and the boxes were from a beauty supply chain. The results came together nicely, but offered a price challenge when replicating the idea.*

CAPSULE

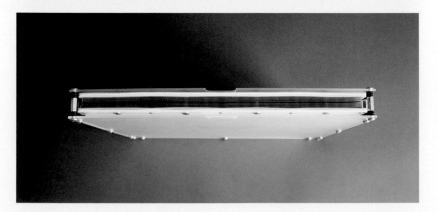

◄▲ *Who says the way in which you house your portfolio has to be boring? WORKtoDATE uses an innovative packaging system for their portfolio, including an industrial-style plastic casing and a handy set of dog tags. These dynamic materials also allow for modification of the portfolio contents to meet the interests of the audience.*

WORKTODATE

# MAKE IT PORTABLE

Be sure to make your portfolio portable so you can always carry it with you. You can always supplement it with a promo kit—those leave-behind gems that are teeming with samples of your work, testimonials, client list, biographical information, and press materials.

"I see less and less conventional books in favor of more thoughtful/creative presentation formats," says Andrea Cutler, professor of design at Parsons School of Design and owner of Andrea Cutler Design. "There was a time when the standard black binder was ubiquitous and expected. Now when I do portfolio reviews, I see more and more unconventional containers, such as metal boxes and other custom portfolios. Of course, it doesn't mean the work inside is going to be better that the next person's, but it makes that presentation stand out and be memorable in another way, and they tend to be cleaner presentations."

One of the nicest books Cutler has seen was a horizontal 17 × 11-inch (43 × 28 cm) book the designer made himself, using simple binder scrapbook screws. The covers were rubber, the pages were teeming with white space, and the book was organized in a case-study fashion.

"The thing I loved most was the book came with a separate index and table of contents page," Cutler says. "So all the text about the clients, assignments, problem-solving specifics, and materials, were on that index/cover sheet and corresponded with the page number. That kept the pages clutter-free, but the viewer could read about each design project if they needed more info. And, of course, the design work was outstanding."

If you have both paper documents and small artifacts, you might consider using a large three-ring binder with work samples and artifacts slipped into plastic sleeves. Albums or scrapbooks make excellent holders for your portfolio if you want to create a more permanent collection and not return the artifacts to storage.

Most portfolio cases range in size from 8 × 10 inches (20 × 25 cm) to 11 × 17 inches (28 × 43 cm). But keep in mind that a portfolio becomes awkward to carry and to view if it is any larger than the sizes above.

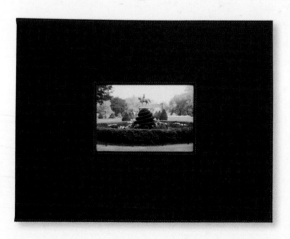

▼ *Traditional leather albums are a perfect way to house some of your key portfolio elements. Soft to the touch, these versatile Lucca books by Kolo offer a luxurious design with wrapped sewn edges in accent thread colors selected to coordinate with the book's lining. Scratch-resistant, water-repellent, and expandable, the Lucca album is lined and offers Kolo's trademark self-contained cover window pocket for portfolio personalization.*

▲ *Inspired by the beautiful design elements of classic premium cigar boxes, Kolo created Kolo Havana Photo Boxes using archival board, European book cloth, and archival bookbinding paper. These handsome boxes feature Kolo's trademark window to hold a photo or label, cleverly positioned on the front side of the box for visibility when displayed on a bookshelf. The large Kolo Havana Photo Box is perfect for portfolios or presentations and is sized to hold two 8½ × 11-inch (22 × 28 cm) albums in coordinating colors and fabrics.*

◄▼ Carrying your portfolio just became a whole lot easier. Oversize yet lightweight, these portfolio cases are versatile, sleek, and offer plenty of room for a medium- or large-size portfolio or laptop. To accommodate a variety of shapes, the cases are available in landscape and portrait styles. They also are fully padded and water resistant. They feature a removable padded shoulder strap, zippered front pocket, and clear ID back pocket.

◄ To dress up your portfolio and provide some extra depth to your presentation materials, this portfolio valise, which measures 15 × 12 × 3 inches (38 × 30 × 8 cm), offers the versatility of a laptop case while also housing samples to show to prospects, clients, or potential employers.

▲ *Portability is key for many portfolios. Bound like a book with linen covers, these small book-style portfolio binders include a sewn spine and accent ribbon tie. Their easy-load pockets hold 24 of your 4 × 6-inch (10 × 15 cm) portfolio images.*

▶ *For digital portfolios, more and more creative professionals are turning to portable digital photo albums. Featuring a slim design encased in a soft leather-like case for a convenient, elegant image display, this photo book offers more than 2½ hours of battery life and an easy and portable way to showcase portfolio images. Ideal for creative professionals to display their work, this photo book supports raw images as well as JPEG, BMP, GIF, and TIF image formats.*

# Promoting Sustainability
## DEMONSTRATING YOUR SKILLS USING LESS

Turn on the television or open a newspaper, and you would be hard-pressed *not* to find information on living green. The sustainable design movement has embraced the global marketplace and captured the attention of consumers like never before. From sustainable building design to alternative fuels to water conservation, entire industries are taking notice and changing the way they're doing business. Even creative professionals looking for sustainable options for their portfolio development have reason to celebrate and can make their portfolio more sustainable.

The sustainable movement is receiving a tremendous amount of attention, so what goes into a portfolio is as important as what goes on it. Soy-based and low-solvent-based corn inks and UV-cured ink technology are very popular. Reclaimed materials—such as fabric and metal—are also being used.

For professionally printed portfolios or self-promotions, people are also minimizing the amount of virgin paper used and are selecting papers that are processed chlorine-free, or that even have seeds embedded in the paper, which can be planted in the ground later to grow flowers.

As for recycled paper, just about every mill offers a paper with at least 30 percent recycled material. Some mills also use alternative energy like wind power.

Today's portfolios and self-promotions run the gamut from simple to grand, from luxurious to subdued. But more and more creative professionals recognize that incorporating environmental elements into their portfolios is more than just green business—it's good business. In fact, for many creatives, sustainability is much more of a standard, as opposed to an exception—they understand the value, responsibility, and profitability of being responsible for the materials and processes they use.

In addition to using more earth-friendly materials, consider engaging your audience in other unique ways. Perhaps you can send a well-designed epostcard or small printed postcard that illustrates your creative genius, while pointing the recipient to your website or blog to learn more about your product, services, and experience. When presenting your work, consider using a portable digital portfolio rather than a printed one. All of these combined efforts can make a significant impact on your company's carbon footprint.

► *Larsen's monthly enewsletter, inSights, demonstrates Larsen's thought leadership via topics of interest to marketing managers, creative directors, and others who need ideas for communicating effectively to target audiences. It is also a wonderful sustainable approach to keeping in touch with client and prospects.*
LARSEN

# LARSEN

> forward to a colleague
> subscribe to inSights

DESIGN
BRANDING
MARKETING
INTERACTIVE

## inSights

no. 32 | 16 December 2008

## Color
### Five trends important to your business

Who's responsible for color trends? Who decides what the next hot color will be? Sometimes it seems as though a fashion designer in a Manhattan loft sits down with a Pantone book and determines for the rest of us what color is in and what color is out. Nothing could be farther from the truth. Color trends actually start from the bottom up — as a reaction to the world around us. Although the fashion industry unquestionably plays a role in color trends, it's also very reactionary, and one of the few industries where color choices change yearly.

Color has an undeniably powerful impact. It reflects and defines our world, and plays a large role in our behavior, emotional responses, and moods. Because of this, it's important for organizations large and small to pay attention to color forecasts and consider color carefully. Here are five trends that can help you make smart color choices for your business.

▸ read the full story

### Color in motion

They asked for buzz. We gave them a brass band. This marketing promotion uses color to attract attention and generate excitement.

▸ view solution

## news

### New work, new clients

Larsen is pleased to announce new branding, design, marketing, interactive, and environmental graphics initiatives for clients including Best Buy, Catalyst Community Partners, Cold Spring Granite, College of Saint Benedict/Saint John's University, Core-Mark International, Fairview, Lominger International, Maple Grove Hospital, MTS Systems, San Jose State University, University of Minnesota, and Wausau Paper.

### Larsen Design Scholarships: 2008-09 Awards

Larsen proudly announces three new Larsen Design Scholars: Elizabeth Berschneider, multimedia design, UW-Stout; Ben Moren, interactive media, Minneapolis College of Art and Design; and Sarah Mytych, graphic design, University of Minnesota-Twin Cities.

▸ read more

## contact

Interested in hearing a Larsen speaker?
We have experts on design, branding, marketing, interactive.

▸ submit your request

IMPLEM

# ENTING

"YOU DON'T MAKE PROGRESS BY
STANDING ON THE SIDELINES,
WHIMPERING AND COMPLAINING.
YOU MAKE PROGRESS BY
IMPLEMENTING IDEAS."
—SHIRLEY HUFSTEDDLER

IT'S 2012: DO YOU KNOW HOW YOUR COMPANY IS PERFORMING? PREDICTING THE FUTURE IS LIKE FORECASTING THE WEATHER. YOU THINK YOU KNOW WHAT'S GOING TO HAPPEN—THEN IT DOESN'T. UNFORESEEN CIRCUMSTANCES AND NONEVALUATED RISKS ARE INHERENT COMPONENTS OF DOING BUSINESS. BUT BY PROPERLY IMPLEMENTING YOUR PORTFOLIO AND SELF-PROMOTIONS, YOU CAN HELP USHER IN A PROMISING TOMORROW.

# Schedule and Budget

Scheduling time to create a portfolio is probably the biggest challenge designers face because time is money. It's time to determine the resources it may require to create your portfolio or self-promotion. How much time can be allocated to developing your portfolio? What is your budget? Remember, you have to spend money to make money.

Look for the most cost-effective avenue for your portfolio development. List all of the methods and materials you would like to use within your portfolio. Break down the costs of each in terms of creating and implementing these materials.

Depending on your workload, formal portfolios, such as capabilities brochures, may be updated annually. Employability portfolios, aimed at landing a job or an internship, might be created throughout the year, and modified for a particular audience.

Utilizing a solid marketing plan, which includes a detailed schedule of upcoming self-promotions and direct-mail campaigns, can further ensure that the schedule, timelines, and budget parameters are being met.

Once you determine the approach you want to take in scheduling your portfolio distribution and self-promotion campaign, you can turn your attention to deciding how to promote yourself and to whom (that's where that handy-dandy database comes in).

According to the U.S. Small Business Administration, "Because marketing needs and costs vary widely, there are no simple rules for determining what your marketing budget should be. A popular method with small business owners is to allocate a small percentage of gross sales for the most recent year. This usually amounts to about two percent for an existing business."

At Minneapolis-based Capsule, creating, marketing, and distributing the firm's self-promotions, which include eblasts, portfolio presentation materials, and holiday promotions, are typically allocated 5 to 10 percent of the firm's revenues each year.

And while you certainly don't want to bombard your designated audience with all-too-frequent promotions, you want to make sure you avoid the adage, "Out of sight, out of mind." Blogs, eblasts, and newsletters can ensure that you remain "front and center." Determine what your clients and prospects positively respond to. For some, it may be graphic-filled eblasts, for others it may be a high-end portfolio brochure, mailed in a contemporary, costly vellum envelope. Whatever the method, choose an appropriate timetable for distribution.

| TYPE | FREQUENCY | | | |
|------|-----------|---|---|---|
|      | Weekly | Twice a Month | Montly | Annually |
| Eblast | | × | | |
| Postcard | | | × | |
| Newsletter | | | × | |
| Portfolio/brochure | | | | × |
| Holiday promotion | | | | × |
| Website update | | | × | |
| Interactive portfolio CD | | | | × |
| Blog | × | | | |

► *A translucent frosted glass portfolio features Organic Grid's logo identity etched into the glass cover. A screw-post binding system makes it easy to swap individual printed samples of the firm's work based on a particular client and their immediate needs.*
ORGANIC GRID

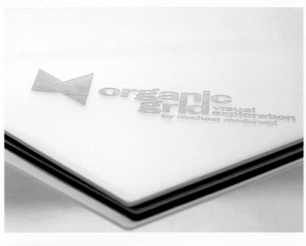

# Presenting Your Portfolio

## IT'S TIME FOR THE SHOWCASE SHOWDOWN

Bring your personality but check your attitude with the doorman. This is the time to show your confidence, but keep far from arrogance if you want to find a receptive audience. There's nothing more humbling than walking into a situation, thinking you know everything and finding out you know nothing. Start from a state of knowing nothing and let your portfolio speak to how much you know. Gain knowledge from each situation and either apply it right away or investigate further and add new tidbits of knowledge in the next presentation.

Presenting is theater: You are the actor, your portfolio is a prop, and the setting is your stage. No detail should be left unconsidered. Your audience will notice everything, even if they never say a word. From a broken seam to a weak piece of work, consider what they will see and what it will mean about you.

Now that you get the metaphor, put it to work. What happens if you spend the first 45 minutes of your hour talking, asking questions, creating some desire to see your portfolio before showing it? All the time leaving it on the table. Build drama instead of doing a portfolio "purge" on the table, putting it all out in front of your audience in the first 5 minutes. Not good theater.

Your portfolio becomes slightly less important if you consider the theatrical approach. Details, like where are your hands and eyes, are two critical pieces of any human communication. Do you let the audience touch your work? Do you create exclusivity by handling each piece with two hands? Consider the moments and you might find yourself spending some time at the theater to get some ideas. Avoid the Greek tragedies.

◀▶ *The StressDesign viewbook is used as an introductory piece for new and prospective clients. The sixty-page book is a showcase of the three main specialty areas at StressDesign: print, publication, and Web design. In order to present their portfolio of work properly, StressDesign clearly identifies the work completed and the overview of the project scope and solution.*

*The firm also offers a smaller eight-page version of the viewbook. It is used as a stand-alone publication for new and prospective clients or as a leave-behind at job fairs or speaking events.*

## WHAT TO INCLUDE

When presenting your portfolio, be sure to include the who, what, how, and why:

··· Who was the client?

··· What was the "problem" that you were hired to solve?

··· How did you go about solving it?

··· Why did you use the design methodology that you did?

Never stumble on the basics. Who is your audience? What's important to them? Who was the client? What problems have you solved? How did you do it? Why did you take a particular approach? What were the results? Simple questions you can outline about each piece of work you are presenting.

Know the answers in your heart, and your passion for the work will come through. If you don't know, say so. Bluffing has many more risks than saying "I don't know."

▲ The well-defined elements throughout the viewbook offer readers a clear understanding of the approach StressDesign utilized with each profiled project.

# Digital vs. Personal

WHAT'S YOUR STYLE?

As Michael Eckersley, principal at Human Centered, a U.S.-based team of affiliated designers, social scientists, and planners, explains, most design today involves plenty of teamwork; the portfolio presentation must be descriptive of that process and credit others on the project. He believes that portfolios today are most useful and accessible online. "Imagery must be contextualized as to project profile, role descriptions, and project outcomes," Eckersley says. "Effective portfolios I deal with today involve video and storytelling, not simply static imagery."

Dale Bohnert, manager of design and communications for 3M Brand Identity at 3M in St. Paul, Minnesota, says that while portfolio presentations have become more electronic or virtual in nature, he prefers portfolio presentations in person, rather than via email.

"The digital age has made it all too easy, too impersonal," Bohnert says. "I find it most appealing when someone says, 'Let's get together and think.' Sharpie markers and napkins—particularly on-the-fly—still impress me more than PDFs."

That said, strategic design, service design, and interaction design require different kinds of portfolio representation than traditional portfolios—say, for graphic design, industrial design, or interior design. "The purpose of the portfolio is simply to rapidly demonstrate competency and quality of creative thinking," Eckersley says. "It shouldn't be lorded over and turned into the equivalent of a fetish object. The portfolio should be shown and put away—not obsessed over. Then the conversation should be steered toward what the client or employer is looking for in the future—not what work has been done in the past in different situations, for different people."

# Ask the Experts

EMPLOYABILITY FACTOR OF TODAY'S PORTFOLIOS

Brett Lovelady, chief instigator at Astro Studios in San Francisco, sees his fair share of designers' portfolios cross his desk. So how do today's portfolios need to function to help land that "oh-so-perfect" job?

"I believe portfolios have taken on a stronger 'personal branding' approach," Lovelady says. "Design yourself a logo or 'logoize' your name with colors to create a more commercial 'you.' The portfolios should be full of process and philosophies in addition to polished results. Create a

Lovelady says that entertainment plays a large role in portfolios, including big, memorable ideas, headlines, unique bios, images, or videos with music.

book, brochure, mailer, website, reel (or some combination if not all), send them out, email a link or PDF, blog or tweet about all of it. Just make it about you, your personality, your point of view, and include your work samples, of course."

"But remember, I don't want to relive your whole project with you," Lovelady says. "Just give me the big ideas and insights—maybe a quirky inspiration image or statement along the way."

At Astro Studios, personal PDFs are appreciated, as are personal websites. Hosted portfolios are also helpful—just as long as they are easy to navigate and not overly "motion" indulgent. "I don't like just slide shows on image sites," Lovelady says. "This seems cheap and less unique—but better than tattered books in most cases. Most importantly, your portfolio is your image-based calling card for instilling confidence in people. It's your insurance policy or pulpit of expertise giving people a sense of who you are, what you can do, what you like to do, and possibly what you can become."

▲ *The use of innovative, contemporary materials helps Bohnsack Design's portfolio book stand out from the crowd.*

BOHNSACK DESIGN

# Distribution Dynamics

## THE KNOCK ON THE DOOR

Formally defined, distribution of your portfolio or self-promotion is the method you use to get your piece into the hands of your designated audience.

Some people feel that you should never leave your portfolio behind at the conclusion of a meeting. Once you let go of your portfolio, you lose control of a key communication tool. Others believe that a portfolio should stand alone and speak for itself.

Depending on the size of your portfolio, you may want to leave a smaller capabilities brochure that captures the core components of your portfolio—something that is a strong advocate for you in your absence.

Do a little recon. Determine what your competitors are doing in the area of portfolio development. Keep tabs on their website content and learn of any innovative strategies you can utilize to keep ahead of the pack.

Pay attention to your database. Okay, so maybe you don't have a database. Get one. To build a fan base, you must build a database of people or

companies who may be interested in who you are and what you have to offer. If you create a phenomenal portfolio mailer but send it to the wrong group of prospects, you have completely wasted your time (and money) and theirs. Ignorance is not bliss. It pays to do your homework. Clichés aside, your mailing list should be those people who believe in what you do.

◄▲► *Akar Studios is a Santa Monica–based multidisciplinary design studio specializing in retail, hospitality, and branding design. They have created a small-size brochure specifically for marketing the retail and restaurant design services of their studio. Displaying an array of projects encompassing bars, restaurants, and high-street retail, the portfolio brochure provides an overview of the expertise the studio offers potential clients.*

AKAR STUDIOS

PLANNING | CREATING | **IMPLEMENTING**

# Making Connections

## GET OUT THERE AND NETWORK WITH THE MASSES

Marketing executives use it as a key tool for their success. Financial consultants use it to obtain new clients and often make it a key part of their overall business strategies. Brand management consultants see it as a necessary effort to expand their business. What is it? It's networking, and in the world of business, people network to help smooth out the potholes on the road to success.

Whether you are the owner of a small design firm or a global firm with offices worldwide, networking with

your portfolio in hand—or at least a mini portfolio—will give you greater leverage than those without it. Those who get out there and flaunt their stuff *have* the ability to gain notoriety among prospects and clients. Those who sit on the sidelines, waiting for someone to notice them, *have not* embraced a "go-get-'em" attitude that can mean the difference between success and failure.

While networking can be beneficial, how and with whom you network are vital to the success of your

self-promotion efforts. People tend to cluster together based on education, age, race, professional status, and more. The bottom line is that we tend to hang out with people who have experiences or perspectives similar to ours. Often, most of our friends and associates are friends and associates with each other as well. The problem with this is that when we surround ourselves with people who have similar contacts, it may be difficult to make connections with new people or the companies we desire to do business with.

◄▲ *This portfolio was sent to various design companies worldwide from Changzhi Lee, a student at Nanyang Tech University in Singapore who was seeking an internship. Because these companies had environmental sustainability as one of their key philosophies, a pop-up book made out of leftover paper was the statement behind the package design. In addition to the curriculum vitae, each package also includes a CD containing samples of Lee's design.*

CHANGZHI LEE

## NETWORKING STRATEGIES

So what are some of the best networking techniques as they relate to portfolio design and development? Try some of these simple ways to network and see where it takes your business.

- **Make a good first impression.** Look good. If you look good, you sell good. Your appearance and attitude do make a big difference, and this is what people see first.

- **Evaluate your surroundings.** Attend an organization's events and interview existing members. Ask them what they like about being a member and their

strategy for getting the most out of their membership. Also, assess what benefits—both tangible and intangible—you will receive for your membership and event fees.

- **Diversify, diversity, diversify.** You need breadth and depth. Participate in different kinds of groups.

- **Work on those referrals.** Referrals are, and will be for the foreseeable future, all about relationships. Whether they're relationships built online or face to face, they're still relationships. People refer people they know

and trust. They won't regularly refer someone just because they're listed on a website—that's called advertising, not networking.

- **Don't oversell.** Bring business cards only. Don't come with brochures, pamphlets, and gimmicks. People don't want to carry these materials around with them. They will most likely throw them away or just set them down and forget to pick them back up.

- **Learn how to "work" meetings.** It's not called "net-sit" or "net-eat," it's called "network." Learn networking systems and techniques

that apply to the different kinds of organizations you attend.

- **Develop your contact spheres.** These are groups of business professionals who have a symbiotic or compatible, noncompetitive relationship with you. In any networking situation, look to make two or three solid contacts whom you can learn from—both from a personal and business perspective. Do not just hop from one person to the next trying to collect as many business cards as possible. That is counterproductive.

- **Create a feeling of trust.** Experts agree that the approach to networking must be about building relationships based on providing value and gaining the trust of others. It is not about getting immediate business. Not enough business owners realize this, and they go into networking with the mind-set of getting business instead of building relationships.

- **Know your goal.** Perhaps most important, understand that networking is more about farming than it is about hunting. It's about cultivating relationships that can lead to productive experiences in the future.

- **Look at whom you know.** Ask your colleagues how you can better promote their business and if they would feel comfortable promoting yours. Join forces with other industry players and host an event. By coming together and presenting to prospects, you will all be promoting your own businesses.

- **Be specific about referrals.** Identify specific people to whom you wish to be introduced. Personal introductions can open doors for you that would've otherwise remained closed. If you don't know the name of the manager of another business you wish to meet, find out—then ask specifically for a referral to that person.

- **Meet one on one.** To deepen the relationships within your network, meet with each person away from the general networking session, to dial up the focus of your networking efforts.

▲ *A streamlined, well-defined portfolio system provides a cohesive message to your prospects and clients. Subtract Studio De Creation is a creative studio encompassing a full range of creative and technical needs in one complete package. This complete package of experience is housed within a succinct folder design with individual case studies highlighting the studio's experience.*
SUBTRACT STUDIO DE CREATION

# Measuring Your Success

## IT'S A NUMBERS GAME

The phone rings, your email blings—all with messages from prospective clients asking to meet with you to learn more about your core competencies. Perhaps they are interested in rebranding their corporate communications system, or maybe they are simply looking for an updated website. Whatever the reason, when a potential client walks across your company's threshold, what's the likelihood their "browsing" will result in a sale? For many businesses, improving their close ratio is key to a successful future.

In the simplest terms, a close ratio is the number of sales that are booked in relation to the number of opportunities that are presented. For example, if ten potential clients walk into your office and listen to your sales pitch and only five of them purchase your services, then the close ratio would be 50 percent.

One thing we know from talking to consumers of creative services is that price alone is rarely the primary motivator in the purchasing decision—in many studies it ranks as low as ninth or tenth. That's true whether you're in a high-, medium-, or low-price niche. So whether you're selling high-end packaging design or discount websites, the purchasing decision is part of a complex formula rooted in how clients know and understand your company, and the products and services you offer in terms of both quality and confidence—all of which should be carefully incorporated into your portfolio and self-promotional materials.

You should also consider tapping into your existing client base—many of whom may be more valuable than you realize. The beautiful thing about having an accurate database of existing clients is that these people know other people. Assuming you offered a gratifying client experience, there is no reason that your old clients wouldn't refer your offering to potential new clients. Perhaps you send out a dedicated mailer to your account base that offers up a small gift for any new clients that they refer to your business. This will give you more visibility and more opportunity for success.

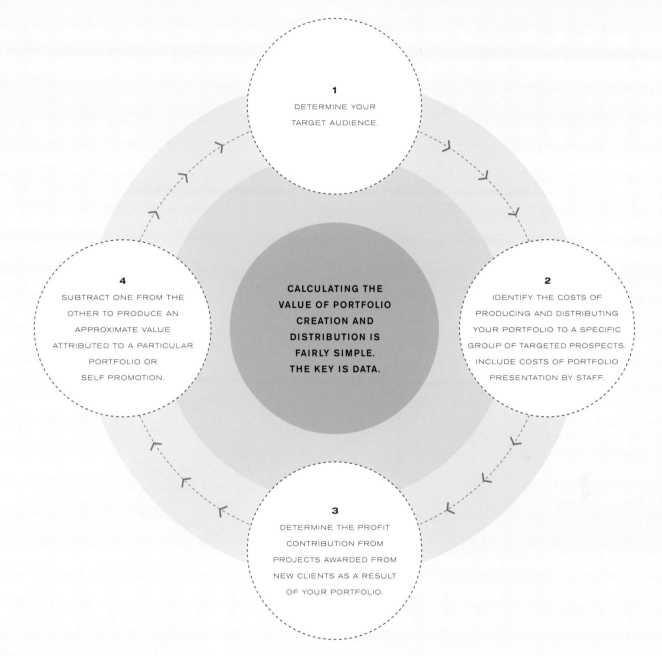

**1**

DETERMINE YOUR
TARGET AUDIENCE.

**CALCULATING THE
VALUE OF PORTFOLIO
CREATION AND
DISTRIBUTION IS
FAIRLY SIMPLE.
THE KEY IS DATA.**

**2**

IDENTIFY THE COSTS OF
PRODUCING AND DISTRIBUTING
YOUR PORTFOLIO TO A SPECIFIC
GROUP OF TARGETED PROSPECTS.
INCLUDE COSTS OF PORTFOLIO
PRESENTATION BY STAFF.

**3**

DETERMINE THE PROFIT
CONTRIBUTION FROM
PROJECTS AWARDED FROM
NEW CLIENTS AS A RESULT
OF YOUR PORTFOLIO.

**4**

SUBTRACT ONE FROM THE
OTHER TO PRODUCE AN
APPROXIMATE VALUE
ATTRIBUTED TO A PARTICULAR
PORTFOLIO OR
SELF PROMOTION.

# Keep Them Coming Back for More

## YOU GOT 'EM RIGHT WHERE YOU WANT 'EM

In the creative industry, it's all about getting people to remember your business, your products and services, and your brand. For many creative firms and individuals, portfolio design is the arena that puts the "big picture" perspective into focus and determines where a company takes and makes its future. It's the philosophy and core behind all business development for many creatives. With that said, more and more business owners are realizing the important role portfolios and self-promotions play in making immediate and lasting impressions on their bottom line.

While creating a solid portfolio and self-promotion program does not happen overnight, you can implement some simple techniques that will make immediate improvements to your clients' experience.

More and more creative professionals recognize that they need to make the portfolio experience as memorable as possible—to help them stand out from the crowd and compete with the big players. While many companies design great experiences, companies often lack the discipline to consistently execute them. To be successful, a company needs to define the experience, create the appropriate tools, train the staff to execute it, and measure its impact on the customer.

- **Create a memorable experience.** Creative professionals can make the experience memorable each time they visit your office or you present your portfolios by finding unique ways to roll out the red carpet, such as addressing each potential client by name, offering personalized parking if possible, and having a lovely room with coffee, water, and healthy snacks available for those waiting.

- **Commit to wow!** Creative firms can really stand out from the pack by coming up with strategies that will truly wow their potential clients and get them talking. Some ideas? Reserved parking, personalized gifts, overnight service, last-minute emergency service, personalized welcome signs for expected clients, and stress-release kits.

- **Partner with other suppliers.** Often clients are overwhelmed with the intricacies of purchasing creative services. Go beyond the business card table, partner with other suppliers, and be a resource for your customers for everything they could possibly need.

- **Survey former customers.** One of the best ways to improve your customer service is by surveying former clients. This means setting up a system to connect with customers and ask them two simple questions: What was your experience like? How can we improve our service? It can be done by phone, by mail, or online. The system produces a numerical rating you can use to measure how well your company is doing. It will also generate useful feedback about what you're doing well and what you need to change.

- **Write a handwritten thank-you note.** Creative professionals can mentally think through every little aspect of their client's experience and come up with ways to wow them at every turn.

- **Publish your customer service standards.** Make sure your employees and your customers know what your customer service standards are. Put them on wall posters, put them on the back of business cards—anywhere clients and employees will see them.

◄▼► *Willoughby Design utilizes two "lookbooks" to showcase the company's portfolio of work. The smaller lookbook is designed for first-time exchanges with potential new clients. The larger lookbook showcases the company's values, creative process, and the most relevant work. Each book is specifically edited to match a client's industry or particular needs. The modular format allows for continuous updating and customization.*

WILLOUGHBY DESIGN

# The Quickest Ways to Kill a Sale

CAN'T SAY WE DIDN'T WARN YOU

Creative professionals are largely in charge of their own destiny. You've found the perfect niche within the industry, honed your creative skills, trained your employees, made your portfolio look perfect, invested in advertising, and are now ready for some serious sales. But sales mistakes can dramatically affect your bottom line. Here are some key mistakes to avoid during the portfolio presentation and sales process:

- **Not listening to a customer's needs.** Selling is more about listening than it is about talking. One of the inherent mistakes many creative professionals make is not listening to a client's request. Listening to and pinpointing exactly what the customer wants will help streamline the sales process and enhance your referral business.

- **Overselling.** We think the more a potential customer knows about a particular product or service, the more likely she will buy the product. In reality, though, information overload has the opposite effect: Instead of leading to a sale, it may lead to an exit—especially if a customer is overwhelmed with information.

- **Improper employee training.** Your best clients have formed an image in their minds of what you are, what you do, and how well you do it. But all of that can be quickly undone by a misguided employee. Your employees are the walking, talking billboards for your business. Every time someone in your company comes in contact with others—whether they are customers or vendors—he or she leaves a lasting impression of your company's brand on their minds. Be sure to train employees to conduct themselves in a manner consistent with your brand message and they will be goodwill ambassadors to your current and prospective clients.

- **Lack of follow-up communication.** One of the biggest mistakes creative agencies and individuals make is forgetting to communicate with their customers after the project has concluded. However, this is a key communication point and sales opportunity. Remember, your customers often spend a considerable amount of time and money with you—you owe them a "thank you" and you owe your company a chance to communicate with the client one more time.

After presenting your portfolio, take the time to write a handwritten thank you note. That's right, the good old-fashioned thank-you written on your company letterhead or personalized stationery. Be sure to thank your prospective client or employer for taking the time to review your portfolio. Don't waste time reiterating your exemplary talent and services. Rather, make it short, sweet, and to the point.

Again, thank them for the opportunity to present your portfolio and ask if they have any additional questions. The resulting conversation will give you a good idea if you made the cut. Of course, if you don't make it, ask why. Inquire about what your portfolio may be lacking and how it compared to others. Taking the initiative to improve your portfolio presentation will illustrate to a prospective client or employee that you take your portfolio seriously.

As Vince Lombardi said, "Some of us will do our jobs well and some will not, but we all will be judged by only one thing—the result."

If your prospect hasn't given you a timeline for getting back to you, give them a call about a week after your portfolio presentation. That way, your portfolio will still be fresh in their mind, and you won't appear desperate.

Keep developing your sales skills to ensure that you have done all that you can for your customer—your future depends on it.

Introduce yourself.

↓

Listen to prospective client's needs.

↓

Justify your experience.

↓

Show your credibility through visuals and testimonials.

↓

Discuss the specific project or job.

↓

Ask for the sale or job.

↓

Schedule the next steps.

↓

Send a thank-you note and repeat your request for the business or job.

# CASE S

DESIGN MATTERS // PORTFOLIOS 01

# TUDIES

"AN ARTIST'S JOB IS TO SEE. AND TO GO OUT IN THE WORLD AND SEE IT FIRSTHAND, JUST AS IT IS; TO REPORT WITH LINE AND WORDS WHAT IS SEEN. TO BE IN THE WORLD, NOT JUST STUDY ABOUT THE WORLD, THAT IS THE ARTIST'S TASK."

—ROBERT FULGHUM

DESIGN FIRM:  FUSION HILL (USA)

# Making Waves and Charting a New Territory with a Unique Portfolio Design

Using a combination of research, strategy, and design, Minneapolis-based Fusion Hill strives to create some of the most innovative, thoughtful design solutions for their clients.

## PLANNING

Fusion Hill attended a networking event in spring 2008 in which marketing materials were not required or even recommended for distribution. Event attendees did not have the ability to carry portfolios or large giveaways from meeting to meeting. That left Fusion Hill in a conundrum: Come up with a way to leave a subtle impression on the potential clients who would be attending the networking event, while differentiating Fusion Hill from the competitors who would also be showcasing their wares.

"Because we were in the travel setting—namely, a cruise ship, we considered luggage tags and ID cases, but it didn't really give us the opportunity to package our story," says Kasey Worrell Hatzung, principal at Fusion Hill. "We wanted to create a product that was uniquely ours. Most other items we considered were already created and really only allowed us to 'brand' them with our logo or colors. We did consider using or giving away products that we had helped to brand or develop from other clients, like a Vera Bradley ID wallet or a food product from General Mills, but they weren't as small, didn't tell our whole story, and were often not unisex or they did not reflect everyone's taste."

▲ Whimsical and inviting, the exterior design of the Fusion Hill tin was indicative of the contents within.

◄ Some of the best things come in small packages. The recipients of Fusion Hill's treasure-filled tin were treated to more than a few savory mints. They were surprised to find a mini portfolio creatively constructed to fit within the confines of the compact tin container.

## CREATING

Because the event was being held on a cruise ship, the design team at Fusion Hill decided to incorporate a nautical theme into their promotional piece—a stainless steel tin of mints. They also wanted to give away something small enough to fit in a pocket, useful enough to keep and use over time, and clever enough to be memorable.

"We also thought of other candies such as gum and chocolates, but again, the mints seemed most useful and the tins would be recognizable as such, then leaving the little portfolio inside as the surprise," Hatzung says. "We found a lot of different-size tins, but we needed it to be able to house a business card and our portfolio, fit candies, and match other materials we were creating for our portfolio. Also, the portfolio inside had to be big enough to show our capabilities and samples of our work but just be a teaser."

While the Fusion Hill team discovered a lot of vendors that will print on a tin or personalize the tins and provide the mints for you, they simply weren't satisfied with what they found. "The printing samples we found were really subpar for a four-color image," Hatzung says.

Recipients were treated to a surprise when they opened the mints—a tiny accordion-folded portfolio with multiple panels that highlighted the key categories of work and industries that Fusion Hill serves, including financial, health care, consumer packaged goods, and women.

Fusion Hill had multiple renditions of the label—all fitting within a certain style. "We were looking for place-based imagery that was fresh, used our colors, but wasn't too wintry as we were sending/handing these out in early spring," Hatzung says.

At one point in the preliminary design process, the labels featured a moose in the distance. "But it felt a little too kitschy and not quite 'us,' Hatzung explains. "We did keep the idea of the 'winds of change' with the cloud blowing. We really wanted this tin to look like a product and not just a branded Fusion Hill mint tin, so we gave it lots of personality."

▲ Some of Fusion Hill's preliminary designs illustrate their direction of celebrating the atmosphere of the northern climes of Minnesota, where Fusion Hill is located, while playing on the minty freshness of the candies themselves.

They branded the product "Wave Makers"—the double entendre plays off being out at sea and the idea that Fusion Hill could deliver change and impact for those ready for a new perspective. Of those attending, Fusion Hill was the only firm from Minnesota, so they wanted to play on that a bit—poking fun at themselves and their frosty climate.

Fusion Hill also chose a tin with an aluminum finish to match an oversize tin that they sent as a follow-up to prospects with their full-size portfolio included inside.

"We also needed to make sure that the mints were protected from the portfolio and for it not to feel tampered with—so we included a vellum wrap that covered the mints and added a layer between the portfolio and a business card we inserted. We then closed the tin with a clear wafer seal," Hatzung says. "Our team wore hairnets and latex gloves and put all the mint tins together in assembly-line fashion at our office."

The mints are wrapped with a little frosted vellum that says "dive in," and once you've depleted the contents and reached the bottom, there is a message that says "hungry for more?" with Fusion Hill's contact information.

## IMPLEMENTING

A first "wave" of forty tins was handed out in person at the networking event. An additional 350 tins were mailed out to prospects and clients. Fusion Hill made a version for clients with customized messaging. The mailer included a clear pouch with the tins floating inside (for visual effect and protection).

"We love the personality of the artwork that uses our corporate blue and strong elements like the waves and the name Wave Makers," Hatzung says. "We like how the whole approach sets us apart from the competition and being new on the scene (for this event), heralds our location and then takes the time to introduce who we are with quick snippets and examples. We packed everything we wanted into a tiny little presentation."

Sending out the "second wave" of their portfolio to clients and prospects after the first event also proved to be very beneficial. "Because we weren't handing them out personally, we needed a unique method of transport. Our mission is always impeccable and creative presentation and packaging," Hatzung says. "We took what is a heavy-looking little tin and made it look light as air by fugitive gluing it inside a clear pillow pack. It just floated inside that pack with nothing but clear air around it."

The mailing label and stamp all fit on a 2 × 3.75-inch (5 × 9 cm) label that was adhered to the pillow pack on the back of the label so that as you looked at the package from the front you didn't see any of the mailing clutter.

"Because any printing and packaging we found from vendors was such low quality, we had our own labels printed on a durable, sticky substrate that could withstand the bumps we knew it would encounter in pockets and purses and still look great," Hatzung says.

The total run with both versions was 650 quantity, and costs for production and supplies (printing of labels, inserts, mints, and assembly) was $1,650, with an additional $500 for postage. "This was one of our least expensive mailers by far," Hatzung says. "Our holiday mailings in past years have been closer to $10 with a similar quantity."

The overall response to the tins was very positive—in fact, many recipients requested more. They were also a great conversation starter for follow-up phone calls—people remembered receiving them and easily recalled the design firm.

"When we handed them out, people of course just thought we were giving them mints," Hatzung says. "We'd tell them there was a tiny portfolio inside, and they would look at us with surprise and start guessing what it might look like or what form it was in, and they'd just have to open them up right there. To us the idea of a portfolio and a giveaway was just the criteria of doing it at all, but people just loved it and thought it was so unique. I think the quality of the finishes, printing, layering, candies, and messages made it really stand out from other standard giveaways we saw. The ability to package so much punch and personality in such a small vehicle proved ingenious."

▲ *To entice each recipient to open the self-promotional tin, each tin was housed in a clear envelope that both enticed and engaged the recipient.*

DESIGN FIRM:  LARSEN

# Celebrating the Historical Passion for Design

With offices in San Francisco and Minneapolis, Larsen creates identities, marketing collateral, websites, packaging, and a plethora of other design elements that help organizations establish or enhance their presence in the marketplace.

## PLANNING

Over the past thirty-four years, Larsen has developed a significant body of work and a reputation for environmental graphics—a unique medium not accommodated by many graphic design firms, and one that can be difficult to demonstrate. "To reproduce images of the work that are representative of its scale, we launched our current brochure series by designing a larger format piece (9.5 × 11.5 inches [24.1 × 29.2 cm]) that feels more like a magazine," says Tim Larsen, principal at Larsen Design. "When first handing it out, we gained an immediate increase in environmental design inquiries, mainly from clients who didn't know we had the expertise."

For Larsen, the firm's printed brochures serve as the primary component of their portfolio system. "We categorize the brochures based on wanting to present an overview of Larsen's current broad range of work (general capabilities), and to highlight specialties within our suite of services (particularly environmental graphics and identity design)," Larsen says. "On occasion, we also feature a particular industry of work from which we are interested in acquiring more business, such as retail."

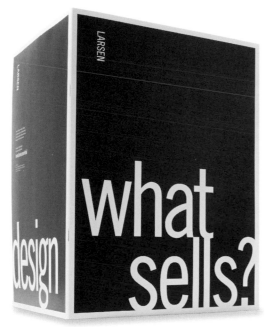

▲ With the redesign of Larsen's own identity, the company adapted a crisp, white look and feel to all of its marketing materials and expanded its arsenal of capabilities literature to include brochures specific to identity design and environmental graphics.

▲ Larsen's experience can be focused in specific industry segments, and the team was excited to promote recent work in retail and consumer products. To address the inherently louder, more assertive sales environment, this piece features large type and even bigger visuals for immediate impact.

## CREATING

The firm's core portfolio was initially bound by metal rivets, so pages could easily be removed and replaced when appropriate. Since the metal scratched the brochures stacked above and below, the firm substituted white plastic rivets for the second piece in Larsen's promotional literature series—the ID brochure.

"This second component was developed based on a lesson learned: It is difficult to show a single identity design alone; identities are best displayed in quantity," Larsen says. With a compendium brochure, Larsen can demonstrate their breadth of visual solutions for identities and give the client a chance to consider a variety of directions. And since Larsen identifies itself as a consulting office, not a style office, a compendium exhibits a diversity of approaches executed by the firm's sixteen graphic designers.

One would expect a general capabilities piece to be the first brochure Larsen might develop. "With our clients, it's easier to demonstrate print collateral by showing actual finished samples," Larsen says. "They exemplify the quality of design, printing, paper, and texture for which Larsen is known. By the same token, we are better able to show our interactive design capabilities by directing prospects to URLs we've designed and developed. Therefore, the two easiest areas to promote—print and interactive—have been the last to be solved through printed literature."

Larsen created the "What Sells" retail brochure to distribute during the recent recessionary economy. "It cuts to the message and demonstrates that we have the ability to help corporations and marketing managers drive revenue to the top and bottom line," Larsen says. "Its brightly colored cover with large type and all full-page photos is a departure from the rest of the promotional literature system, primarily because B2C requires a more assertive approach than B2B."

▲ *Every month, a new project is featured in a large-format postcard, with a single thought and image on the front and a case study on the back. This direct mail is sent as a memory tickler to Larsen's client and prospect mailing list.*

## IMPLEMENTING

Larsen's printed brochures are primarily given to serious prospects and clients with whom they anticipate working. "In the past, we may have sent brochures to an extensive prospect list due to its low cost, but now that we print fewer pieces and they cost more per item, we are fairly selective as to who receives them," Larsen says. "We occasionally send literature to a short list of companies in a particular industry we want to pursue, or send individual targeted packages that address news about a company that fits with our experience."

Each component within Larsen's portfolio arsenal has been designed by a different Larsen designer, with Larsen serving as creative director in every case.

The current literature system printing cost is about $18 to $20 apiece based on digital, short-run (250 pieces) printing. The unit cost of previous years' examples was $8 to $10 each, but when printed in quantities of thousands, Larsen couldn't use the brochures in a timely manner and the featured work became dated.

▲ *With its extensive portfolio of identity designs, Larsen built a card deck that could include all or some of the exemplary work based on what a client wants to see— and bound together by a rivet.*

"The goal of our promotional literature is to gain new business and referrals from existing clients, past clients, recommenders, partners, and prospects," Larsen says. "The purpose of the literature has been to exhibit our client work—rather than be a statement about design itself. In many ways, we have taken our cues for the layout of the pieces from publications like *Communication Arts* and *Graphis*." As the viewer flips though the brochure, it has a design annual feel—clean, straightforward images and minimal text. This familiar format makes it comfortable to view the work. As a result, the pieces came together easily and quickly in terms of the design process.

High-quality photography has always been a crucial element to the design (from signage to packaging to print), so Larsen has budgeted for it every year and art-directed professional studio photographers. They are then able to use these images in their Web portfolio, for case studies, and for archival purposes.

Another major decision was choosing the paper and binding method of the brochures, as Larsen wants to display top-quality materials and methods. "Our binding system has evolved from PVC to spiral to perfect binding, and more recently rivets in metal, then plastic," Larsen says. "Today, we are utilizing a match-cover style of stitching the book and folding over the cover to hide the stitches."

With the advent of the Web came significant change, however. "For many clients, printed pieces have become a supplement, and in some cases are not necessary when they can see our portfolio online," Larsen says. "Nonetheless, it's reassuring to have a leave-behind or a tangible item to mail in order to elicit a meeting. Additionally, the demographics of the final decision maker often require a variety of media for up-channel selling."

It goes without saying that every printed piece Larsen produces includes their URL so the prospect or client can locate the firm's online presence to quickly assess their abilities and access their contact information.

"An informal survey indicates people appreciate the books, which offer a chance to look at Larsen's work in depth at their leisure, and as a resource when projects arise," Larsen says. "The brochures are viewed as gifts rather than promotions because they make good reference tools that demonstrate excellence in design."

◄▼ *To celebrate the company's twenty-fifth year in business, the image of a paper airplane (an adjunct element to the Larsen identity at the time) was set into motion in a flipbook that invited clients, prospects, partners, vendors, and friends to "Soar with Us."*

DESIGN FIRM: OLOGIE (USA)

# Setting the Stage for Success

Ologie understands what it takes to tell a good story by exploring creative avenues that will lead to smart brand solutions for their clients. Based in Columbus, Ohio, Ologie inspires a myriad of creatives, including designers, writers, researchers, planners, and strategists to develop the best outcomes for their clients.

## PLANNING

Cohesiveness. It's an important element in many facets of life. Interior designers embrace it. Sports team managers strive for it. Medical specialists would be lost without it. It creates a symbiotic relationship among people or elements that defines who they are and what they do. And when an individual or firm is looking to promote themselves, creating a cohesive design for their portfolio materials is paramount. Just ask Ologie, a Brooklyn-based design firm that strives to provide a consistent message in who they are and what they do.

"When determining how to categorize our portfolio system, we separated the big buckets of information clients wanted to know," says Beverly Bethge, partner at Ologie. "We looked at how businesses talk about themselves and make themselves more digestible, so we divided our portfolio contents into three distinct categories:

- "Skill Set: What we do

- "Get Set: How we do it; our approach

- "Mind Set: How we think about it, our point of view."

◄ *Each element within the Ologie portfolio components follows a similar theme, design, and layout. Complementary yet distinct, the Skill Set, Get Set, and Mind Set elements offer a comprehensive look into Ologie's offerings.*

► *With the Get Set piece, the Ologie team thought it was important to tell clients what they're about to get into, and why this commitment of time and money is worth it. "There's a business equation on the other side," Bethge says. "The work we do is a huge catalyst for change in their organization. They need to know that. This piece gets them to see the totality of their brand, as opposed to tactics they might associate with branding, such as an ad campaign or a logo."*

Skill Set outlines exactly what Ologie does, without any jargon. "When you have key people in the business who have been at it for more than twenty years, there's a certain point of view and confidence that you can't change even if you wanted to," Bethge says. "It's how you go to work every day. If you put it out there and are honest with clients, they respond to it."

▶ Mind Set is more of a character piece. It's as much an internal piece as it is an external one. If there's one document that can rally everyone in the company to deliver on-brand, this is it. "It's not a detailed process manual about how we do things," Bethge says. "It's more about how you feel about things. We're so clear on our mind-set that it took less than 10 minutes to write and was completely unedited. If a client gets through these pieces and believes in what we believe in, if they believe in the approach and think great work can come from it, if they're entertained by our style, then it's going to be great."

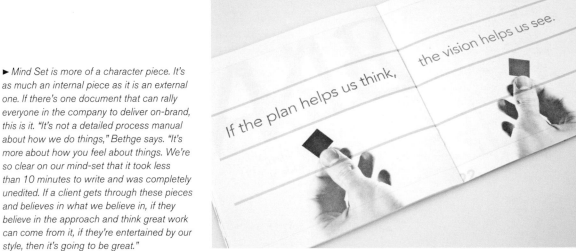

## CREATING

A huge part of the Ologie experience is about simplification—which is very different from being simplistic. "We simplify big, chaotic messes," Bethge says. "A lot of firms say that, but we deliver it. And our space and our collateral communicate that immediately."

The Ologie team wanted these pieces to look beautiful and make perfect sense to the user—because that's an Ologie-like experience. They also know that size matters, so the pieces are interesting sizes.

Also, in an age where every presentation is digital, Ologie still believes in leaving something tactile behind. "People like to hold something that's real," Bethge says. "We believe it makes everything more tangible. And more credible."

▲ Each of the categories within Ologie's portfolio system means something. "To have put them into one brochure would have been too much for people to get through. And it would have been boring," Bethge says. "So we tried to give people a different way to access that information. Plus, it's like a gift, and recipients want to explore it. We're rewarding them for wanting to get to know us."

People take action with their heart.

# AND THAT REQUIRES A VERY DELIBERATE APPROACH ON YOUR PART.

ologie

FINAN
SERVIC
INTAN

But that doesn't mean financial

## IMPLEMENTING

Ologie's introductory pieces are given to prospective clients, visitors, partners, vendors, presentation attendees—many different audiences. But as the Ologie team gets to know prospective clients, and better understand their needs, they put together more customized presentations that feature case studies of situations similar to theirs.

"Clients are always fascinated by the vinyl folder with the orange *O*s all over it," Bethge says. "One client even requested something similar for their brand."

Bethge notes that advisors are always telling Ologie to specialize in a single industry. "We think that's boring. And besides, you learn so much from one industry that you can apply to another. For example, we're constantly using retail tactics in financial services," she explains.

▲ *Three of Ologie's magazines—B2B, Greater Good, and Financial Services—all feature the work the firm has done for these industry segments. Following a distinctive design strategy, these three publications entice the reader with streamlined and engaging copy.*

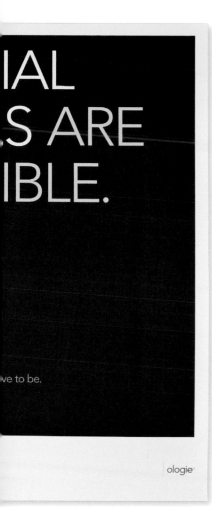

# BUSINESS-TO-BUSINESS MARKETING CAN BE COMPLEX.

Which is exactly why your story should be simple.

ologie

But Ologie's prospects and clients always ask, "How much experience do you have in my industry?" So they put together a set of magazines to send out to current and prospective clients to show their expertise in specific categories, such as B2B, financial services, nonprofit, and higher education. "The magazines share our design and photography capabilities through the layout of the pieces, but really highlight case studies through a feature-story approach," Bethge says. The magazines quickly deliver Ologie's perspective and experience with the industry. Ologie has only made one round of minor edits to two of the pieces within their portfolio system, developed three years ago.

"Whenever you look back on everything, you're bound to find something you want to change," Bethge says. "But as we look through these pieces, they still reflect exactly who we are. And we couldn't be prouder of that."

DESIGN FIRM: INTEREUROPE COMMUNICATIONS GROUP
(ICG, UNITED KINGDOM)

# Separating Themselves from the Pack

From design and public relations to advertising and new media, Intereurope Communications Group (ICG) is a "one-stop shop" for clients who are passionate about strategy, design, and getting their message out there.

## PLANNING

As part of its new-business drive, ICG has historically sent out various brochures to businesses to gain account wins. "However, through follow-up calls we discovered that our brochures were not gaining the attention of decision makers," says Simon Couchman, creative director at ICG. "Simply asking 'do you remember the blue brochure?' wasn't working, as marketing managers receive so much material from agencies." In addition, ICG's online presence was weak, with little content. They needed a new system that stood out from other agencies, yet wasn't so overdesigned that it weakened the creative work they were trying to show.

"Through initial research, we recognized that despite designers opting to present their company portfolios using the latest fashionable typefaces, special inks, and finishes, they were inadvertently distilling the actual work they were trying to present," Couchman says. "We therefore identified that we needed a system that was very clean and graphic, retained a strong identity, and at the same time didn't dominate the work we deliver to clients."

ICG's second step was to focus on the services that they offer and wanted to promote. They included their four distinctive services—graphic design, public relations, new media, and advertising—all under the umbrella of one company. "We therefore retained our existing corporate logo, but muted the colors to a single warm gray, and typographically we chose a classic: Helvetica Neue."

◄▼ *Using the ICG stripes motif,* The ICG Bumper Book of Client Case Studies *offers an in-depth look at some of the projects that have helped ICG make a name for itself.*

## CREATING

To support and reflect the individual services, ICG introduced a set of four brightly colored stripes, which were assigned to each service. "This reflected our position as an integrated full-service agency and at the same time defined the individual services that we provide," Couchman says.

To support this striking appearance, they also started to include a device in their mailings to help people remember the portfolio items they sent out. Currently, it's a lollipop made from Blackpool Rock, a type of rock candy made in Blackpool, England. The lollipop features the ICG stripes, reflecting their location close to Blackpool itself. In addition, a sticker on the lollipop states: "Our rates take some licking…" which gives readers an immediate insight into ICG's cost structure.

"Once the core corporate brochure was agreed and developed, we then transferred the look, feel, and selected content to other promotional devices, such as our websites," Couchman says.

ICG initially considered the implementation process from a commercial perspective, asking themselves, "What do we want to sell to the marketplace?" "What messages do we want to convey to potential clients?" and "How do we effectively present this information?"

"We looked at a lot of agencies' promotional material, as well as our current brochures, and reviewed what we liked and didn't like," Couchman says. "Our house style is generally colorful, clean, uncluttered designs that communicate clearly and effectively, so we looked at using an uncluttered graphical treatment."

Influences included Farrow's designs for the Pet Shop Boys' *Introspective* album, and the Penguin book covers of the '60s. "The stripes answered our requirements," Couchman says. "Once the idea was there, it was hard to shake. We experimented with various colors and chose a vibrant selection that would stand out on people's desks and yet would work in harmony."

ICG also wanted to reflect their strategic approach and included many of the services they offer. They chose case studies with a range of strategic commercial and communication objectives, such as increasing sales. These examples would interest marketing managers and company directors.

"We presented the case studies uniformly, so that from both a copy and visual perspective they clearly explained the project or campaign challenges—as well as the creative solutions and results," Couchman says. These creative solutions were illustrated by a mix of studio-shot photography and flat spreads.

◄▲ *Each year, ICG creates an annual book reflecting on and celebrating the firm's creative accomplishments during the previous twelve months. Each month consists of one or two significant events, including projects completed, awards received, or results of a public relations campaign for a specific client. This annual book illustrates the breadth and depth of ICG.*

## IMPLEMENTING

ICG's portfolio consists of a twenty-page, large-format case study brochure titled *The ICG Bumper Book of Client Case Studies* and sixteen-page pocket-size guidebooks to the firm's various individual services, as well as an activity-review mini brochure. The portfolio theme is carried out through additional promotional pieces, including a twenty-four-page public relations case study brochure, *The ICG Little Black Book of Public Relations and Copywriting*, specially manufactured holiday gifts, two blogs, and two websites.

The initial design process, including the design of the main brochure, took about a month to complete. ICG continues to update case studies and other components on a regular basis to keep materials fresh—particularly on the websites and blogs.

"The system has evolved over the last twelve months, and as the stripes are becoming more recognized, we are able to have fun pushing what we do with them a little more," Couchman says. "We had a client arrive for a meeting in the striped hat and scarf we sent out as a Christmas gift this winter. She's hoping we do gloves next."

ICG's in-house capabilities allow the firm to self-publish some of their mini guides when they need to communicate with potential clients. "For example, we have just sent out a small guide that talks about marketing during a recession," Couchman says. "These enable us to responsively communicate current issues and reflect our understanding of the challenges that companies face."

All of ICG's materials have had to be extremely cost-effective, so where possible, the ICG team undertakes work themselves, including the website build, all photography, and digital printing of the mini guides.

▲▶ *ICG is an award-winning full-service agency, offering clients four distinctive services, including graphic design, public relations, new media, and advertising. To promote these separate disciplines, the firm devised a set of four brightly colored stripes and assigned each service its own color (for example, orange for graphic design). The branding is simple yet effective and has been rolled out across all elements of ICG's promotional material—from stationery, business cards, and website to corporate brochures and their annual "highlights" books. It is also included on a number of promotional items, including mugs, scarves, lollipops, and even the firm's interior office décor. The simplicity of the vibrant stripes ensures consistency and creates a core brand for the agency without having to "overdesign" their own material.*

"Our strong relationships with printers enables us to have the main brochure litho-printed at a good cost," Couchman says. "We generally print around 2,000 copies of the main brochure at a time, with updates to the case studies when we reprint."

ICG also found a great supplier of the hats and scarves. The supplier can source wool in the exact colors in the system, and can produce them as ICG needs them. "Our lollipops were specially made by a local manufacturer, who even let us select our own flavor," Couchman says.

ICG distributes the elements of their portfolio differently:

• Potential clients will initially receive the brochures, along with a lollipop.

When they go to meetings, ICG's business cards and presentation continue the striped theme.

• Current clients will regularly receive the mini guides and newsletters, in addition to their day-to-day communications.

• At Christmas, ICG mails all clients their winter gift: a hat and scarf, along with the "highlights of the year" book.

"The response has been overwhelmingly positive, with an increase in new business appointments," Couchman says. "When following up prospects, the lollipop acts as a great prompt, and often we will get requests for additional lollies for clients' children. We have also received a few photos of clients on skiing holidays wearing our hats."

DESIGN FIRM: CACAO DESIGN (ITALY)

# Multidimensional Portfolio Design

Founded in 2004 by Masa Magnoni, Alessandro Floridia, and Mauro Pastore, Cacao Design strives to satisfy their clients' integrated communication needs. Working with clients across a myriad of industries, Cacao Design specializes in corporate identity and Web design.

## PLANNING

Italian design—clothing, art, textiles, and architecture—has long been celebrated as the epitome of high-end design. Clean lines, impeccable materials, and awe-inspiring artistic renderings make Italian design elements some of the most sought after in the world. The same can be said for the portfolio brochure produced by Cacao Design. Based in Milan, Italy, Cacao Design has created a unique piece of art in their firm's recent portfolio.

"'The nonconventional brochure is an object to play with while turning over the pages," says Mauro Pastore, cofounder and creative director at Cacao Design. "This is what we always try to do when we work on our clients' brochures: change classic printed pieces of paper into designed objects. Our brochure incites an emotional response and displays the real substance of our creativity and work approach, which is to come up with unexpected solutions that speak directly to the client's heart. Enjoy your brand!"

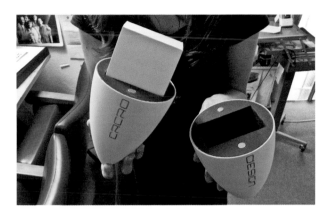

Initially, the Cacao Design team fell in love with another idea: a small-size brochure that, when closed, was about the size of a deck of playing cards with full-page photos of their work inside. "This precious little 'pit' was placed inside a big seed that reproduces our logo in 3-D, revealing the concept: cacao seed, fruit of desire, synonymous with savor and passion," Pastore says.

But as the planning process evolved, they decided to utilize a dimensional Plexiglas exterior with an etching of the firm's motto, "enjoy your brand."

## CREATING

Cacao Design is very specific about their graphic choices for each project. "We pay meticulous attention to artistic detail as it relates to the brand, to create an emotional connection with the target audience before their brains process the message," Pastore says. "Words are not enough to transmit the meaning of what we do and how we do it." Their portfolio includes examples of these projects done for various clients.

What's more, the Cacao Design brochure had to present the firm's print communication projects, showcasing not only their creativity, but their attention to print and production details.

"The format in which we present our portfolio satisfies our need to demonstrate our design abilities by revealing aesthetic, smart, and functional design," Pastore says. "We chose not to use captions in our photographs but, rather, allow our clients to realize our ability to thrill, amaze, and innovate."

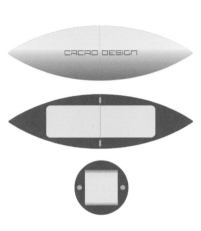

◀▲ *Cacao Design wanted to create a work of art to house their portfolio. These preliminary design ideas and prototypes incorporate Cacao's identity elements to effectively present their portfolio.*

▲ *The aim of this exceptionally designed portfolio is to demonstrate the depth of research, the attention to detail, and the passion that go into each of Cacao Design's creations.*

## IMPLEMENTING

For more than two years, the portfolio brochure has accompanied every presentation that Cacao Design has done, and unless it is upon the client's request, they do not bring examples of other work.

"We leave our brochure with the client," Pastore says. "We rarely mail it, because we like to interact personally and see the first reaction of the client when he or she opens it. Plus, mailing the brochure would be too costly." In fact, the cost of producing each portfolio (including shoot, preprinting, and printing) is about about $140 (£126) each.

"Our brochure is an object that surely positions the agency on a higher level than those found in the industry standards. It's targeted to clients who can appreciate and afford high-level brand designs," explains Pastore.

▲► *As an example of Cacao Design's unique way of approaching design, they show the art direction of the "still life" photos focusing on their outstanding creative solutions, care for details, and avant-garde printing techniques. Cacao's portfolio book emphasizes the creative energy and spirit that rings true for staff and clients alike.*

DESIGN FIRM: NATIONAL FOREST DESIGN (USA)

# Seeing the Forest through the Trees

## PLANNING

What do you get when you cross high-end creative projects for such clients as Nike and Urban Outfitters with exceptional photography and illustrative copy? An outstanding portfolio for National Forest Design in Glendale, California, an award-winning, full-service creative think tank with an expertise in execution.

"We create visual languages that can last a season or a lifetime," says Justin Krietenmeyer, art director at National Forest.

National Forest's mission is to design without limits, as explained in its "concepts and executions" portfolio book: "We push and pull at the cultural fringe. We bounce our ideas off thoughts, and innovations off executions. This is what we have to offer—our combination of passion, personal commitment, fearless creativity, and innovation."

To capture this mission, the National Forest team sought to create a book that effortlessly embraced their successes in the field of design, while illustrating this "new brand of creative agency."

What's more, National Forest sought to create a portfolio book that showed the team's inherent knowledge of today's subcultures with their unparalleled expertise in graphic execution.

Each page within the National Forest portfolio book is a treasure to behold—teeming with innovative design concepts, all of which are presented in an authentic, powerful way. Filled with a wealth of case studies, the book celebrates the intrinsic values that National Forest utilizes to create their innovative concepts.

Before we're designers, we're inspired.

Welcome.

## CREATING

National Forest created a portfolio book that clearly illustrates specific projects, approaches, and results featuring a variety of design styles. The ninety-page, perfect-bound portfolio book with a heavyweight bond paper dust jacket features three case studies and a handful of projects the firm recently completed.

"The National Forest book is for our clients and prospective clients, to demonstrate our capabilities as a design firm," Krietenmeyer says. "The design rationale is fairly straightforward. We have a small introduction discussing our thoughts as a design studio and its responsibilities within the world of art, marketing, and design."

The book then goes into three case studies of larger projects the firm has worked on with Nike, Element Skateboards, and Urban Outfitters. After the case studies, the book includes a handful of other projects that showcase National Forest's capabilities.

▲ *Each page within the portfolio book is strategically designed in such a way that it depicts the visual elements used in designing a project from concept to release.*

## IMPLEMENTING

"Our concepts and executions book is sent out regularly to new and potential clients," Krietenmeyer says. In the book you will find a range of creative projects from an Urban Outfitters catalog, to a mural at Rudy's Barbershop in downtown Los Angeles, to a variety of action sports gear and apparel.

"We have experience with every type of design—from physical products to print ads, music festival posters, branding books, and catalogs," Krietenmeyer says. "In addition, we have taken on a number of projects from start to finish: art direction, photography, and design, so we wanted to include as much of this work in the book as possible. We sent out a couple hundred when we first got them," he says. At a cost of $45 each, National Forest probably only sends two or three a month these days—mainly to companies who are thinking of working with National.

In addition to their portfolio book, they created a demolition derby car as an art and marketing experiment. "We decided it would be interesting to purchase a car, paint it, and enter it in the demolition derby that takes place in Irwindale, California," Krietenmeyer explains. Their race team, the West Coast Rippers, ultimately raced the car and lost.

DEMOLITION DERBY                    Selected Projects

A National Forest graphic experiment. After creating the race team "The West Coast Rippers," National Forest purchased, designed, entered, and sponsored a demolition derby car for the destructive enjoyment of all in attendance. The National Forest demolition car competed and lost at NASCAR's world famous Irwindale Speedway on June 17th 2006.

84

85

"We made posters, T-shirts, and pit passes. We bought a block of tickets and invited more than 150 friends, family, and clients to come see the carnage. We liked the idea of creating a somewhat serious collateral package for such a wacky event," he says. "It was a fun time, even though our car lost very early on."

Every five years or so, National Forest updates their portfolio components. "As we have only made this one book, I am not sure what we will do next time—probably more of a printed art piece than a catalog of client projects," he says. "The books have been received well. It is hard to tell what actually brings in the work, but we have been busy and steadily growing as a firm."

▲ Using the medium of a demolition derby car, National Forest cleverly advertised and subsequently destroyed their artistic self-promotion—but had a blast doing it!

DESIGN FIRM: ALPHABET ARM DESIGN (USA)

# The ABCs of Portfolio Design

As a full-service design firm, Boston-based Alphabet Arm Design is a full-service design studio specializing in bold, creative, and distinctive print design solutions including logo design, branding, collateral design, CD art direction, and merchandise design.

## PLANNING

At Alphabet Arm, they take self-promotion seriously. Well, like a seriously funny joke. Their studio environment is very focused on producing high-quality work, all while having as much fun as possible.

"Our portfolio is an ever-evolving and changing collection of materials to promote the various services that Alphabet Arm offers," says Aaron Belyea, art director at Alphabet Arm. "When we create a new promotional piece, we always bring that 'fun' attitude to the table so that we can be sure that it represents the studio when we aren't there to speak for ourselves."

Alphabet Arm also looks at self-promotion as an opportunity to work on projects that they might not be able to do through their normal clients. As a result, they work to create items such as stickers and badges that they enjoy collecting from other people.

"Our materials are very targeted in their message, though the actual goal varies," Belyea says. "We begin the design process with a clear concept in mind and with the objective of addressing a particular need. Taking the logo mini brochure as an example, we felt we needed a self-contained booklet that would showcase a wide range of identities that we've designed over the years. The piece was directed at more of a business audience than some our other promotions, while at the same time being consistent with the voice that we have established for the studio."

## CREATING

In most cases, Alphabet Arm's promotional portfolio pieces are very focused in that they are designed to fill a specific niche. "While the final aesthetic decisions remain open, the idea that we want to communicate is often quite well formed from the beginning," Belyea says. "Similarly, due to the frequency at which we produce materials, most of the ideas we have end up being produced in some form or another."

Though Alphabet Arm uses them in many situations, several promotional pieces in particular make up the core of their patented "Sample Pak." "The Sample Pak was created soon after the studio's inception when we quickly realized that the sooner a potential client could see what we do and how we do it—in a fun, interesting, physical format—the better," Belyea says. "From that point, it was generally an easy leap for them to contract our services for their projects. Basically, it was our way of taking graphic design—an increasingly more esoteric field—and making it really clear and accessible to potential clients."

▲ Concise and small in size, Alphabet Arm's portfolio components use a fun, whimsical approach to "getting the word out" about this multifaceted firm.

And while the design is different for each promotion, Alphabet Arm has several overall design principles that they always work around. "First and foremost, the design needs to be organized and clear," Belyea says. "We are very aware that our clients—who are often unfamiliar with the design process—benefit from having more information about what we do and how we do it. We also made sure that the information remains central to the design, and that it is not obscured by the format."

## IMPLEMENTING

Two factors determine the size and format of Alphabet Arm's promotional pieces: envelope size and cost. "Due to the size of the envelope, we are always aware that the finished piece needs to fit inside," Belyea says. "Costwise, each piece needs to remain as economical as possible. Though we know that each piece's life span will certainly justify its cost, we try to stretch our self-promotion budget as far as humanly possible."

The firm's promotional portfolio isn't distributed at any regular interval, but they do often bring Sample Paks to networking events and client meetings. "We have found that they are excellent conversation starters and nice leave-behinds," Belyea says. "Sample Paks don't always stay in the hands of their original recipient, but often get passed around between clients, coworkers, and peers, so it also becomes an excellent referral tool for us. Finally, we have a form set up on our website that lets anybody request a Sample Pak. It has gotten to the point where we've had to restrict requests to the U.S., as we were getting too many people asking for them from abroad."

Alphabet Arm has been in the fortunate position to offset the cost of some of these pieces by partnering with a number of select printers. "We have designed joint promotional pieces with these partners, and have also been strategic in working them into press runs for other jobs," Belyea says. "That said, production costs vary from $1,000 to $2,500 (£606 to £1,515) per run." Several thousand pieces are printed at any given time.

During Alphabet Arm's eight years of existence, the firm's promotional Sample Pak has been very successful, with two or three new pieces being added annually. "We continually hear from people that it is an excellent resource and it has helped to convince clients that we are the right studio for the job," he says. "It has also helped to get word out about our studio, since we are fairly small in the grand scheme of things, and don't have a large budget for our own marketing and publicity." And when Belyea and the rest of the Alphabet Arm team is there to hand out the Sample Paks in person, people are often amazed at all of the parts and pieces that come in it.

"Once they get a few moments to take everything in, they love the attitude and humor that we put into each piece," Belyea says. "From the feedback that we've gotten, it seems that our message is coming across loud and clear."

DESIGN FIRM: GO WELSH (USA)

# A Passion for Unique Portfolio Presentations

With dozens of projects featured in a wealth of different publications, Go Welsh has earned a reputation within the design community for creating innovative, inspiring branding and design initiatives for clients and for their own firm's promotional materials.

## PLANNING

Go Welsh's main goal for their portfolio was to approach the design in a way that would allow them to cost-effectively create a series of themed promotional pieces. "We had talked about four-color offset printing but felt we'd be limited by production costs in terms of the final size (dimensions) and length (number of pages)," says Go Welsh founder Craig Welsh. "We really liked the idea of being able to work at a larger scale across many more pages than we'd realistically be able to afford on an ongoing basis with offset printing. We had also produced some newsprint-based pieces for a client and found that the tactile, low-grade quality of the paper and inks was a nice change from the slickened world of hi-def, screen-based media. It has an authenticity that's hard to find in other materials. It's the medium from which the masses used to get their news."

## CREATING

According to Welsh, the most difficult task was to come up with a title for the publication. "We had many, many concepts we reviewed over the course of several weeks. However, every title we considered brought its own unique set of emotional and implicit messaging," Welsh says. "We didn't want the first issue to set a mood that would be challenging to address with future issues. So we finally started to seriously consider *Title* as the title with the ability to clearly theme each issue."

▶ *A treasure trove of sorts, Title 01, the "Thanks" issue, was sent by Go Welsh to family, friends, clients, and prospects.*

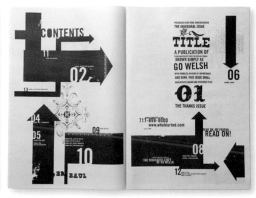

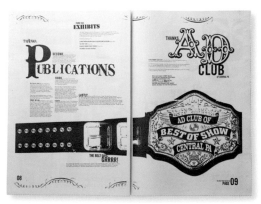

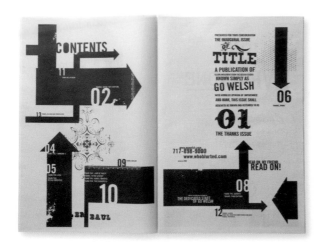

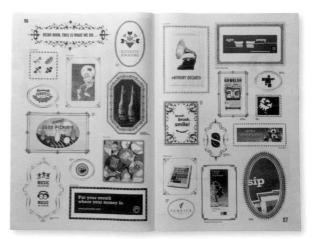

*Title* won, and the theme for the first issue was "The Thanks Issue." *Title* 02 was "The Giving Issue." The flexibility of theming is paramount, and the future issues in the works will include "The Alphabet Issue" and "The Contributor Issue."

Go Welsh also wanted to highlight the firm's writing capabilities in these promotions. "We're a design studio, which tends to make people think we only work with visual elements," Welsh says. "We expect our designers to also have solid writing skills, and *Title* has provided an outlet for writing. Each issue includes contributions from all of our staff, regardless of their role within the studio. The issues are truly expressions of everyone here. In fact, we had a high school intern contribute several elements to *Title* 02."

### IMPLEMENTING

The goal of these newspaper-style portfolio pieces is to get people to stop and take notice. "To help aid in that, we do a few things beyond simply designing and printing each issue of *Title*," Welsh says. "First, we write all the addresses by hand. We have a total of about 900 addresses—our staff LOVES to do this. We like that it has a more personal feeling when it hits someone's desk, as so few pieces of mail are addressed by hand these days. Second, we create a rubber stamp that is applied to the outside of the envelope that is unique to each issue." The stamp for *Title* 01 read, "You Might Want to Open This in Private," and *Title* 02 included, "Give It Up for [arrow]" above the recipient's name.

Go Welsh sends *Title* about once a year, each issue costing about $0.25 to print. "We'd like to send them more frequently, but we've been busy with client work and we're so particular and picky with how we design *Title* that it usually takes a long period of time to complete," Welsh says. The firm sends issues to family, friends, clients, prospects, and pretty much anyone who asks for copies. After posting an image on their website of *Title* 02, they had people emailing from all over the United States and someone in London also requested to be on the mailing list. "We've also distributed several hundred copies at presentations we've given. They usually get grabbed up pretty quickly—funny how excited people get about newsprint."

Go Welsh has had two people call to talk about projects simply based on their reactions to the "Give It Up for…" stamp. "One has since turned into a new client," he says. "We also have a current client that has pinned the envelope to her office wall because she likes the "Give It Up for…" stamp above her name so much."

They also included a full-page puzzle in the last spread. There were 192 triangular shapes mixed up on the left side of the spread with a numbered grid on the right side of spread.

"We got this idea based on work from Norman Ives we had seen in an exhibit," Welsh says. "We like curious people and try to be curious about things when we work. We wanted to see if anyone would take the time to complete the puzzle. We thought it would only be fitting that 'The Giving Issue' of *Title* would include a prize for the first person to complete the puzzle. We set up a unique email address and waited. And waited. And waited. And around the thirtieth day we finally received an email from someone who had completed the puzzle. The reward for such curiosity was a brand new iPod."

The studio then posted an image of the completed puzzle on their website and began getting calls from other people who were frustrated that they hadn't taken the time to put the puzzle together. However, they also expressed similar reactions along the lines of "I should have known you would do something like that!"

"We had a client tell us a funny story about his teenagers arguing about who gets to sit in the front seat of the car," Welsh said. "Turns out his daughter had hopped in the front passenger seat, buckled in, and thought she had outwitted her brother. However, her brother had read through *Title* 02 and cut out the 'Calling Shotgun' coupon. He proceeded to knock on the front passenger window and held up the coupon to show his sister that he was now claiming shotgun. The dad had also read through *Title* 02 and knew what the coupon was declaring. Holding back laughter, he then honored the coupon and made the daughter get in the backseat so the son could have shotgun. The coupons have been much more fun than we anticipated."

◄▲► *Called* Title 02, *"The Giving Issue,"*
*this self-promotion was distributed prior*
*to the 2008 holiday season. Go Welsh*
*reconfigured previous logo projects into gift*
*wrap patterns. The issue also included a*
*visual puzzle that, when completed, revealed*
*a hidden message with an email address*
*to claim a prize for the first person who*
*completed it.*

DESIGN FIRM: WET DESIGN (USA)

# Making a Systematic Splash

Los Angeles-based WET Design works with developers, architects, and other design visionaries to create truly one-of-a-kind water displays that entice and inspire audiences. From the famed Fountains of Bellagio in Las Vegas to the Winter Olympic Cauldron introduced in Salt Lake City in 2002, WET creates award-winning water features that have won the accolades of thousands.

## PLANNING

WET Design's book, *Elements of Magic*, was conceived to communicate the achievements of WET, an organization whose expertise lies in creating experiences through installations that harness the magic of nature's elements.

The book focuses on expressing the experiential qualities of WET's work. Every page offers a visual feast of vibrant photography contrasted by whimsical drawings that engage on a more intimate level. Color, imagery, copy, and texture synthesize to express the essence of the projects and the brand.

"Conveying a sense of WET's work in an emotional and visceral way is the book's aim," says Nadine Schelbert, director of image and branding at WET. "It is designed to set forth the magical quality that unfolds within the world of WET. The book creates this world in front of our eyes, draws you in, and takes you on a journey."

"Experience, playfulness, and magic were the leading characteristics for the design direction," Schelbert says. "These concepts gave birth to a plethora of ideas: spreads that turn into pink origami terriers, leading to an absurd but memorable dog collection; WET swatches—our equivalent to Pantone swatches—that become stickers for our partners to use in their projects; a glossary of WET terms, overlaid onto portfolio images, magnifying aspects of our experience-centric

▲► Titled "Elements of Magic: Volume 1," this marketing book is designed to communicate the achievements of WET, an organization whose expertise lies in creating experiences through installations that harness the magic of nature's elements. The book follows a nonlinear structure centered on visual expression. Every page offers a feast for the eyes of vibrant photography contrasted with illustrations that engage on an intimate level. Color, imagery, copy, and texture synthesize to express the essence of WET.

thinking; books in the plan-view shape of a project; interactive elements such as water-feature personality wheels, and water-feature choreography templates where our fingers become jets of water."

Finally, the leading thread of the book crystallized in the creation of small, endearing characters—WET people, friends, fans, keepers, etc. The book follows their journey through imaginary worlds where dreamlike water expressions animate their lives.

## CREATING

Through a series of schematic designs, the WET team developed a structure and system that included key components such as featured projects and the WET story, while allowing the work's experiential, playful, and magical qualities to be expressed. The idea of layered content quickly emerged, as this allowed different levels of engagement with the same material.

"Design and copy went through numerous iterations. The book grew in size; its shape morphed from rectilinear to crazy and back to rectilinear, then grew further," Schelbert says. "Leading color schemes went from white to black to gray, to an explosion of color held within monochrome brackets."

Generous and striking imagery, engaging drawings, and copy that evokes people's experience with WET saturate the pages. A comfortable balance between majestic, sensual, and playful is achieved. The experiential quality is further emphasized through tactile materials and processes that catch and reward the senses.

"The book is not a one-time read," Schelbert says. "It unfolds over time, rewarding with continuous discoveries."

The layering of information enables varying degrees of contact with the material and addresses the interest of WET's different audiences. A quick glance offers visual excitement, a further peek captivates senses and imagination, and deeper engagement draws us into the magic of WET's story.

"There is a clear departure from the conventions of design-firm portfolio presentations," Schelbert says. "Architectural and design references and portrayals are put aside in favor of a play with the senses, and immersive experience. Magnified is the encounter with nature's elements, and people's connection with them and with each other."

▲ *Strong imagery throughout the book allows WET's expertise to speak for itself.*

The design of the cover is subtle and silent, and reflects the state of a project before it comes to life. "To the noninitiated, it feels intriguingly beautiful; to all it is pleasingly tactile," Schelbert says. "The hard cover gives the book substance and gravitas and contributes to making it a collectible."

The size, which increased over the course of the design, was chosen to make the book more comfortable to browse through and to accommodate the type of imagery it contains. On the upper size limit, the book had to fit into a standard FedEx envelope; on the lower one, it had to hold letter-size and A4-size inserts.

Papers were chosen for their print and tactile qualities, further enhanced through dull and gloss varnishes, debossing, and foil stamping. Silver accents draw light into the book, and varnishes heighten the impact of the color. All elements converge to convey a sensual feast of sight and touch.

"The book is a rich experience, not aimed at communicating facts, but at creating an impression," Schelbert says. Content categories and sections are abandoned in favor of layered information so that every page is visually stunning. Information is organized so that it is easy to understand and absorb, not overwhelming.

▲ *Clear, crisp images capture the powerful movement of the water designs and draw the viewer into the pages. Short copy provides the select information needed to describe the essence of each project.*

The book holds a folder in the back that engages the space in a three-dimensional way, creating a rewarding unfolding experience. Its motion reflects that of choreographed water and further draws to the experience of WET's work.

## IMPLEMENTING

Printing and binding cost per book is $10 (£6) for a run of 5,000 copies. "Absolute perfection in the production quality was achieved through close collaboration with our printing and binding partners," Schelbert says. "Printing alone took over eighty hours."

"Staccato screening combined with our Heidelberg printing presses was the perfect solution for the WET book," says Anthony Narducci, president of O'Neil Printing in Phoenix, Arizona. "Considering this was our first project with WET, the results speak volumes of the advance planning and partnering to get the very best results."

In the relatively short time since its publication, the book has carved out a niche of its own in the design world. "The immediate reaction is as though we were presenting clients with a precious gift," Schelbert says. "Those who receive it treat it with respect. Upon inspection, they turn page after page, read, and comment. They are grateful and pleased to be included on the select distribution list."

Several clients and prospective clients have called to tell WET that it is the best piece of its kind they have seen in years, and ask if it would be possible to have another copy for one of their associates at their firm. "It has become somewhat of a collector's item, since it best depicts the diversity of WET's projects and stellar impact on audiences worldwide," Schelbert says.

This book is the first in a series that will be issued every six months. "Our aim is to always include a novel idea to make each edition stand out from the others, not just through the addition of the firm's newest projects, but by always revealing a different facet of the firm," Schelbert says. "Our hope is that the set of books become a collector's item."

DESIGN FIRM: AFTERHOURS GROUP (USA AND INDONESIA)

# An Oversize Effort Pays Off

Since 1995, Afterhours Group has created brand identity systems, as well as print and interactive designs, for clients both large and small. With offices in Jakarta, Indonesia, and Denver, Colorado, Afterhours Group has made a name for itself with its award-winning *Yellow+Grey* quarterly newsletter. Aside from Afterhours Denver, the company also has a second design agency called Lightbox Indonesia, and a sister company—Red & White Publishing, which publishes high-quality coffee-table books.

## PLANNING

When the Afterhours Group determined the need for an innovative publication that espoused their stature within the international design community, they brainstormed ways to get their message across.

"We needed a company profile that reflects Afterhours as a very dynamic graphic design company," says creative manager Fefria Martosubroto. "It has to be something fun, interesting, and out of the ordinary. And as a company that keeps growing and evolving, a newsletter that can be updated anytime, seemed to be the perfect solution to represent who we are."

Martosubroto says the name of the newsletter was the first challenge. "We wanted it to be catchy, yet at the same time really reflect who we are," she says. "Many names came up during our brainstorming session, including *A+* and *40 by 60*." The name *Yellow+Grey* was finally chosen because it represents the firm's corporate colors.

## CREATING

The *Yellow+Grey* newsletter consists of two major components: *Yellow*, which talks about Afterhours as a graphic design agency; and *Grey*, which shows the life within Afterhours.

"As this was our company profile, the design had to be very 'Afterhours,'" Martosubroto says. "To show our seriousness and quality of work, the design on the *Yellow* section is kept simple and clean. We applied a more personalized style to the *Grey* section to show the fun and dynamic personality of the firm."

The core component of the *Yellow* section of the newsletter begins with the firm's history—namely, a brief introduction on how Afterhours was formed, its milestones, and achievements. "The name Afterhours itself was chosen because initially it was a business run after office hours by the owner, Lans Brahmantyo, who already had a day job as a graphic designer in an advertising company," Martosubroto says.

Incorporating a case study was also paramount to the newsletter. In one particular edition, Afterhours chose the *Land of Water* project. *Land of Water* is a coffee-table book that shows a pictorial journey of George Tahija and his boat captain, Paul Dean, along the waters of Indonesia starting from the island of Bali to the island of Komodo. The concept of the book was to work as a scrapbook that includes sketches, notes, and photographs of the journey. To make the pages look like a traveler's diary, every page was given effects using Photoshop. Even the text was handwritten and scanned.

▲ *Colorful illustrations and imagery offer a unique glimpse into Afterhours' design expertise. Personal insight is celebrated at Afterhours and can be experienced along the bottom of each spread, each offering a connection to the firm's design team through strategically placed, illustrated profiles of each team member.*

Other pages within the newsletter include those that showcase Afterhours' extensive portfolio, including annual reports, calendars, bottle packaging, posters, marketing collateral, and corporate identities.

"The variety of work displayed in the newsletter shows how Afterhours appreciates every client's identity—thus making each piece different from one another," Martosubroto says.

The *Grey* component features an exterior cover boasting fingerprints of Afterhours' employees. "Our goal in this section was to reveal the activities of the people inside Afterhours, so we thought fingerprints would best represent this," she says. "In every edition, we intend to insert a comical story of the life of a designer in Afterhours. A twist of fate shows the process of handling a project, starting from receiving the brief, searching for ideas, getting the project done, but, unfortunately, at the end finding out that the project is canceled."

The employees of Afterhours are the true voice of the *Grey* section, as demonstrated in *Glimpse*, a section where employees get to write about anything they find inspiring—from great design books to light and funny novels or even music.

"The vision of *Yellow+Grey* is to show Afterhours as a whole," Martosubroto says. "Behind every portfolio we produce, there is always hard work, great ideas, and talented people. That is why we chose to have two sections—one that displays our ability to produce great work, and another that shows the energy and passion of its people."

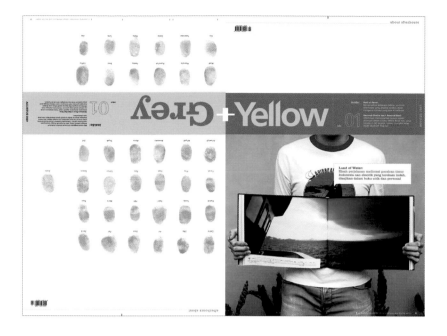

## IMPLEMENTING

The newsletter was initially produced for a yearly event held for the creative industry, attended by professionals in design, photography, printing, and paper. "In an exhibition open to the general public, and creative people in particular, we needed a company profile that would stand out among the crowd," Martosubroto says. "That is why we chose the extra-large but efficient size for printing."

With 2,000 copies printed in the past two years, the newsletter has been distributed not only to existing clients, prospects, and students, but also at art and graphic events.

"The production cost was zero because we partnered with a printer and paper supplier who, in return, were featured within," Martosubroto says. "It's a very subtle joint collaboration. It's all because we have a good relationship with them to be able to exploit everyone's strengths, which normally would cost a fortune." Although the newsletter was intended to be produced quarterly, due to the extensive workload and to preserve the quality of the portfolio shown, the newsletter will be produced only twice a year.

The response to the *Yellow+Grey* newsletter has been very positive. "The large size has always brought admiration, and the use of bright colors and the clarity of the design has made it into an unforgettable company profile," Martosubroto says. "The fact that we also show the daily activities of the employee also helps the audience understand who we are."

▲ *The covers of each side of* Yellow+Grey *artfully reveal the distinct contents within each section. Readers are required to turn the book over to read each section.*

# GALLER

Y

"FIND THE GOOD, IT'S ALL AROUND YOU.
FIND IT, SHOWCASE IT, AND YOU'LL
START BELIEVING IN IT."
—JESSE OWENS

▲ *For easy reference, TFI Envision created a portable portfolio housed in a swatch-book style for easy accessibility and portability.*

TFI ENVISION

◄▼ *Italy-based Gramma created a portfolio product that goes beyond mere self-promotion, to include an experience that consists of colors, sensations, and different elements that usher the viewer to discover something new. The portfolio is contained in a CD, while the brochure features Gramma's story—namely their history and their core capabilities in the area of design.*

GRAMMA

▼ ► *With French-folded pages and stitched binding, this four-color portfolio booklet showcases a series of selected projects and captures the essence of Spark Studio's working environment.*

SPARK STUDIO

▲ New Haven, Connecticut–based Elements created a 2008 holiday self-promotion that features 100 percent Connecticut-made products, including hot cocoa, sugared nuts, honey, and maple syrup. Custom packaged, the items were shipped along with a retro 1950s-themed recipe book containing Elements office favorites and childhood holiday memories.

ELEMENTS

▲► *Dublin-based Dara Creative has created a mini portfolio that speaks for itself. Containing a small selection of the firm's work, the mini portfolio provides a glimpse into what the firm has to offer. Printed on 100 percent recycled paper, the portfolio also contains a spread introducing the Dara Creative team to prospective clients.*

DARA CREATIVE

▲ *Short proposal deadlines often necessitate a virtually instantaneous response on the part of the Quango team. This binder's modular format allows for efficient combination of boilerplate and custom elements into a single, compelling leave-behind. Hand stamped with a custom-made wax seal, each binder is a unique work of art.*

QUANGO

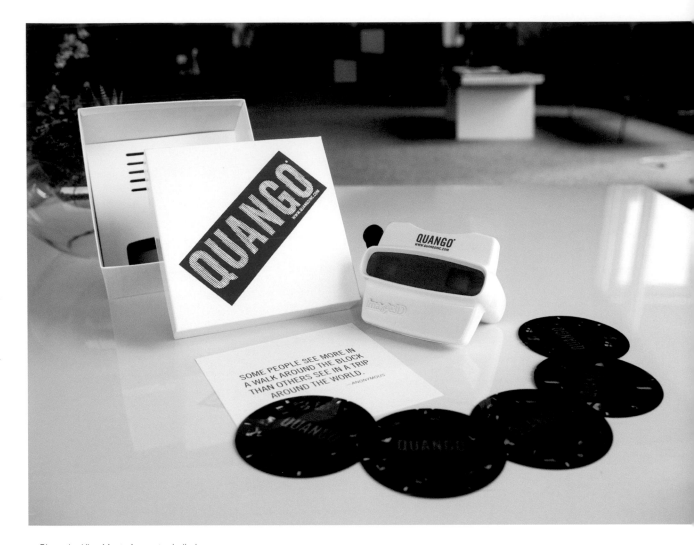

▲ *Since the ViewMaster's creator hailed
from Portland, Oregon, where Quango is
also located, the device was a natural choice
for showcasing scenes from around town.
Three reels feature stereoscopic photos
from Portland's most popular boroughs, and
a fourth includes images from the Quango
offices—for those who have yet to receive
a firsthand tour.*

QUANGO

▲ Everyone needs some relief from holiday stress. Bundling together an eye mask, earplugs, aromatic oils, and an exclusive wine blend in an attractive, reusable lunch box, Quango accompanied the kit with tongue-in-cheek instructions. The lunch boxes received warm welcomes from harried (but soon-to-be-relaxed) recipients.

QUANGO

► *OPX wanted to create an updatable*
*portfolio showcase book for potential clients.*
*The firm created French-folded leaves on*
*gloss and uncoated stocks, die cut and held*
*together with an elastic band.*

OPX

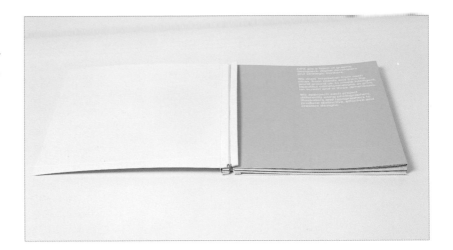

▲ Paragon Marketing Communications in Kuwait has been an agency dedicated to creativity and ultimate customer satisfaction. This promotional calendar transmits that message by comparing creative powers to the most ferocious creatures in the world. The hawk, the ram, the shark, and the bull, to name a few, have their own unique capabilities to survive, and Paragon has adopted these characteristics. The calendar, through each month, conveys the agency's creative sharpness by closely observing and studying the market, the clients, and the competition.

PARAGON MARKETING COMMUNICATIONS

▲ *What's a unique way to showcase more than thirty-five years of corporate identity work? A portfolio in the form of playing cards, of course. Graphic Communication Concepts in Mumbai, India, has utilized a unique medium in which to share the firm's wealth of corporate identity experience.*

GRAPHIC COMMUNICATION CONCEPTS

▼ *This direct-mail box is filled with a hand-assembled, twenty-page fold-out portfolio booklet and was sent to product managers as a congratulations and reminder of all the award-winning packaging and promotion that TFI Envision has designed and produced over the past five years.*

TFI ENVISION

▲ *This self-promotion highlights each area of concentration in the Department of Art at Sam Houston State University in Huntsville, Texas, including ceramic, animation, drawing, graphic design, painting, photography, printmaking, and sculpture. Metallic CD cases containing the art department information appeal to high school audiences, who are generally interested in music. The back of each piece can be used by prospective college recruits for sketching, memos, or notes. The overall production is versatile and cost effective, allowing the art department to add information or change images simply by inserting or removing a sheet.*

DEPARTMENT OF ART,
SAM HOUSTON STATE UNIVERSITY

◄▼ *Showcasing samples of Firebelly's favorite projects, this promotional DVD reel blends graphic design, illustration, and typography into a playful narrative that carries the viewer through the studio's finest work. It also features in-depth case studies and a short documentary about the studio's creative process. Housed in a custom letterpressed envelope, this piece represents a quintessential Firebelly project: culturally relevant, forward thinking, and inspired by Firebelly's illustrious past.*

FIREBELLY

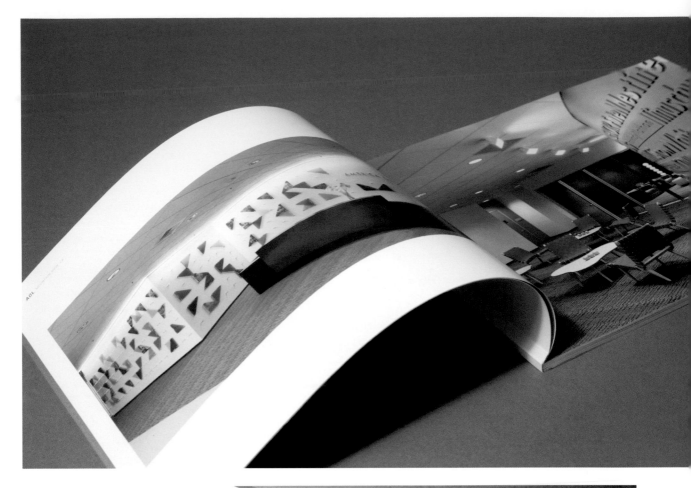

▲▶ *ASD enlisted the help of its graphic design component, Sky Design, to create a comprehensive book of both ASD and Sky Design's capabilities. These books are used to introduce the firm to new clients, to leave with existing clients, and to demonstrate to potential employees the experienced approach ASD and Sky Design take to every project. ASD/Sky Design is a multidisciplinary design firm offering interiors, architecture, and graphic design services to a variety of corporate, financial, restaurant and hospitality, retail, medical, and institutional clients.*

ASD/SKY DESIGN

▲◄ This self-promotional postcard series by Murphy Design, aptly named "Chew on This," is a collaborative effort between the designer Rosemary Murphy, photographer Lisa Godfrey, and writer Susan Hemphill. Sent bimonthly, each postcard featured a different breed of dog, with clever copy correlating the unique traits of each particular breed to the creative traits that these three professionals exude.

MURPHY DESIGN

▲ Christmas is a time of celebration of things that are born in mangers, barns, and stables. Just like New Zealand's Kiwi summer, barbecues and Christmas are meant to go together. Alt Group in Auckland, New Zealand, sent out bottles of wine featuring different animals that, when cooked, pair well together. Recipes are also provided as part of the promotion.

ALT GROUP

# RESOU

# RCES

"WHY SHOULD A CRAFTSMAN NOT MAKE USE OF ALL HIS TOOLS IF THEY WILL PROMOTE A GREATER COMMUNICATION AND EXPRESSIVENESS? THIS IS NOT TO DENY THAT BEAUTIFUL THINGS CAN BE FASHIONED OUT OF VERY MODEST MEANS, BUT WHAT POSSIBLE OBJECTION CAN THERE BE TOWARD AN ARTIST TRYING TO BE MORE RESOURCEFUL?"

—DON ELLIS

## ASSOCIATIONS

**AIGA**
The professional association for design
www.aiga.org

**The Art Directors Club**
The forum for creativity in advertising, interactive media, and design
www.adcglobal.org

**Design Management Institute**
www.dmi.org

**Graphic Artists Guild**
www.graphicartistsguild.org

**Icograda**
The International Council of Graphic Design Associations
www.incograda.org

## BLOGS

*Core77*
Design magazine and blog
www.core77.com

**CR Blog**
News and views on visual communications from the writers of the *Creative Review*
www.creativereview.co.uk/cr-blog

**Design Observer**
Writings about design and culture
www.designobserver.com

**Designers Who Blog**
A design blog for designers, photographers, writers, and marketers who blog
www.designers-who-blog.com

**DesignNotes**
Posts on culture, design, and advertising
http://designnotes.info

GraphicDesignBlog.org
Offering the latest updates regarding the graphic design industry
www.graphicdesignblog.org

## BOOKS

*Building Design Portfolios: Innovative Concepts for Presenting Your Work*
Sara Eisenmann
Rockport Publishers

*Creative Arts Marketing*
Elizabeth Hill
Elsevier Science & Technology Books

*Designing Creative Portfolios*
Gregg Berryman
Skillsoft

*Designing a Digital Portfolio*
Cynthia Baron
New Riders

*The Designer's Guide to Marketing and Pricing: How to Win Clients and What to Charge Them*
Ilise Benun
F+W Media, Inc.

*The Graphic Designer's Guide to Portfolio Design*
Debbie Rose Myers
John Wiley & Sons

*Graphic Design Portfolio Strategies for Print and Digital Media*
Robert Rowe
Prentice Hall

*How to Survive and Prosper as an Artist: Selling Yourself without Selling Your Soul*
Caroll Michels
Henry Holt & Company

*Integrated Marketing Communication: Creative Strategy from Idea to Implementation*
Robyn Blakeman
Rowman & Littleman Publishers, Inc.

*Portfolio Design*
Harold Linton
W. W. Norton & Company

*Ultimate Small Business Marketing Guide*
James Stephenson
Entrepreneur Press

*Web Design: Best Portfolios*
Julius Wiedmann
Taschen America, LLC

## MAGAZINES

*Communication Arts*
www.commarts.com

*Eye*
www.eyemagazine.com

*How*
www.howdesign.com

*I.D.*
www.idonline.com

*Metropolis*
www.metropolis.com

*Print*
www.printmag.com

*Promo*
http://promomagazine.com

## WEBSITES

Behance
A site gathering the portfolios of the artists of the world
www.behance.net

Corporate Design Foundation
A nonprofit education and research organization
www.cdf.org

Creative Latitude
Education and business practices
www.creativelatitude.com

CreativePro
Graphic design software, reviews, news, and resources
www.creativepro.com

The Design Encyclopedia
A user-built guide documenting design
www.thedesignencyclopedia.org

Design Melt Down
Design elements, trends and problems in Web design
www.designmeltdown.com

Design Talk Board
News and reviews about all things design
www.designtalkboard.com

Dexigner
Design portal featuring the latest design news
www.dexigner.com

LinkedIn
Online networking for professionals
www.linkedin.com

CONTR

# BUTORS

"IT IS JUST THAT WE SHOULD BE GRATEFUL, NOT ONLY TO THOSE WITH WHOSE VIEWS WE MAY AGREE, BUT ALSO TO THOSE WHO HAVE EXPRESSED MORE SUPERFICIAL VIEWS; FOR THESE ALSO CONTRIBUTED SOMETHING, BY DEVELOPING BEFORE US THE POWERS OF THOUGHT."

—ARISTOTLE

**LLDESIGN**
Art Director: Lorella Pierdicca
Designer: Lorella Pierdicca
Italy
Page 34–35

**LLOYDS GRAPHIC
DESIGN LTD**
Art Director: Alexander Lloyd
Designer: Alexander Lloyd
Page 68–69

**LOCKSTOFF DESIGN**
Art Director: Susanne Coenen,
  Nicole Slink
Designers: Susanne Coenen,
  Nicole Slink
Germany
Page 24–25

**MMR STUDIO**
Art Director: Dean Teniswood
Designer: Dean Teniswood
Australia
Page 63

**MONDERER DESIGN**
Art Director: Stewart Monderer
Designers: Stewart Monderer,
  Jason Miler, Stuart McCoy,
  Jessica deBry
USA
Page 57

**MURPHY DESIGN**
Art Director: Rosemary Murphy
Designer: Rosemary Murphy
USA
Page 183

**NATIONAL FOREST
DESIGN**
Art Directors: Justin Krietemeyer,
  Steve Harrington
Designers: Justin Krietemeyer,
  Steve Harrington
USA
Page 142–145

**NIKOLAUS SCHMIDT**
Art Director: Nikolaus Schmidt
Designer: Nikolaus Schmidt
Austria
Page 28–29

**THE O GROUP**

Art Directors: Jason B. Cohen,
  J. Kenneth Rothermich
Designer: J. Kenneth Rothermich
Page 10–11

**OLOGIE**
Art Director: Beverly Bethge
DeDesigners: Ologie Design
  Team
USA
Page 126–131

**OPX**
Art Directors: David Bennett,
  Bill Bickerstaff
Designers: Jason Healey,
  David Bennett
United Kingdom
Page 176

**ORGANIC GRID**
Art Director: Michael McDonald
Designer: Michael McDonald
USA
Page 93

**PARAGON MARKETING
COMMUNICATIONS**
Art Director: Louai Alasfahani
Designer: Huzaifa Kakumama
Kuwait
Page 177

**QUANGO, INC.**
Art Directors: Marc Anteparra-
  Naujock, Alec Hill
Designers: Ashley Carter,
  Kristin Wille, Greg Cohen
USA
Page 61, 173–175

**REAL ART DESIGN
GROUP, INC.**
Designers: Real Art Design Team
USA
Page 77

**ROME & GOLD CREATIVE**
Art Director: Lorenzo Romero
Designers: Lorenzo Romero/
  Zeke Sikelianos
USA
Page 72

**SAM HOUSTON
  STATE UNIVERSITY,**

**DEPARTMENT OF ART**
Art Director: Taehee Kim
Designer: Ivan Leung
USA
Page 180

**SPARK STUDIO**
Art Director: Gary Domoney
Designer: Gary Domoney
Australia
Page 59–60, 170

**SPUNK DESIGN
  MACHINE**
Art Director: Jeffrey K. Johnson
Designer: Jeffrey K. Johnson
USA
Page 53

**STEVEN SWINGLER**
Art Director: Steven Swingler
Designer: Steven Swingler
United Kingdom
Page 75

**STRESSDESIGN**
Art Director: Mark Stress
Designer: Mark Stress
USA
Page 94–97

**SUBPLOT DESIGN INC.**
Art Directors: Matthew Clark,
  Roy White
Designer: Ala Pytlewska
Canada
Page 62, 76

**SUBTRACT STUDIO
  DE CREATION**
Art Director: Alistair Maclain
  Stiegmann
Designer: Stephanie Stiegmann
France
Page 105

**TFI ENVISION**
Art Director: Elizabeth P. Bell
Designer: Brien O'Reilly
USA
Page 168, 179

**WET DESIGN**
Art Director: Nadine Schelbert
Designers: Jane Moon,
  Avo Adourian
USA
Page 156–161

**WILLOUGHBY DESIGN**
Art Director: Ann Willoughby
Designers: Willoughby Design
  Team
Page 108–109

**WORKTODATE**
Art Director: Greg Bennett
Designer: Greg Bennett
USA
Page 80

**WORRELL DESIGN**
Art Director: Leo Wang
USA
Page 71

DESIGN MATTERS // PORTFOLIOS 01

191

# About the Author

Maura Keller is a writer and editor based in Minneapolis, Minnesota. She writes about design, marketing, promotions, and a wealth of other topics for a wide range of regional and national publications, as well as Fortune 500 employee communication materials. In addition, Maura provides copywriting and editing services for corporations, advertising firms, and creative agencies.

Her understanding of brand and marketing issues was refined during her years as a marketing communications writer for Yamamoto Moss, an award-winning brand design firm in Minneapolis.

As a writer who is "so into her work that she dreams of creating another letter in the alphabet," Maura has won awards from the Minnesota Society of Professional Journalists and several of her creative writing pieces, including her memoir and poetry, have been published in various literary journals. With a passion for literacy, she serves as vice chair for Read Indeed, a nonprofit literacy program based in Minneapolis.